As I Think About my Savior

A Thought for Each Day of the Year

Philip M. Hudson

Copyright 2016 by Philip M. Hudson.
The book author retains sole copyright to his contributions to this book.

Published 2016.
Printed in the United States of America.

All rights reserved.

No portion of this book may be reproduced, stored in a retrieval system, or transmitted in any form or by any means – electronic, mechanical, photocopy, recording, scanning, or other – except for brief quotations in critical reviews or articles, without the prior written permission of the author.

ISBN 978-1-943650-13 -2

Library of Congress Control Number 2016932545

Illustrations - Google Images.

This book was published by BookCrafters
Parker, Colorado.
bookcrafters@comcast.net

This book may be ordered from
www.bookcrafters.net
and other online bookstores.

As I Think About my Savior

Food for thought, as you think about the Savior each day throughout the year.

Table of Contents

Preface

Introduction..1

As I Think About my Savior...13

About the Author..397

Also by The Author...399

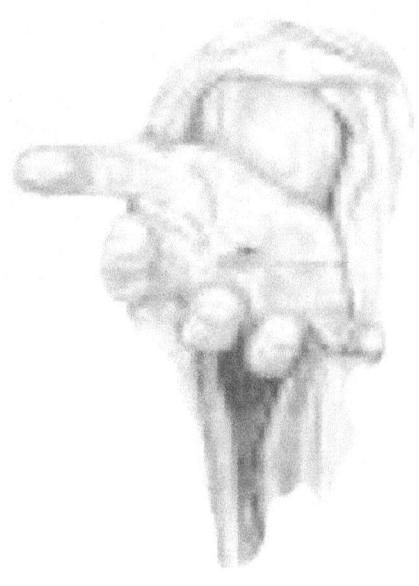

Preface

As we think about our Savior, we are only doing what comes naturally, because we have been hard-wired to seek Him. In fact, there are many who are "kept from the truth (only) because they know not where to find it." (D&C 123:12). This book, then, tries to capture the essence of our innate tendency to be drawn to Him. Its scope is ambitious because it tackles the great questions, but at the same time it asks for a commitment of just one or two minutes daily of consistent contemplation. Its title could have been "Baby Steps," but I was quickly reminded that this disarming invitation had already been used by Dr. Leo Marvin, the noted New York psychiatrist, as the catchy title of his own self-help tutorial.

The unabashed objective of this work has been to seed the atmosphere of our inspiration, so that nurturing moisture might fall upon our tender testimonies of Jesus Christ and facilitate the germination of the seeds of faith that are key to the transformation of our nature. As we think about our Savior, perhaps we will intuitively respond to the invitation to do a little better, to be a little more kind, to be a little more merciful, and a little more forgiving; "to put behind us our weaknesses of the past, and go forth with new energy and increased resolution to improve the world about us, in our homes, in our places of employment," and "in our social activities." (Gordon B. Hinckley).

The structural symmetry of the book's expressions mirrors the coherency of the principles of the Gospel itself, and its format, with 366 entries, invites your daily consideration. While it may seem daunting to embark upon such an undertaking, there was method to my madness, to echo the words of Polonius.

Calendars are interesting devices. They are always with us, patiently waiting in the wings, ready to assist us in our efforts to organize, structure, and balance our lives. Even if we choose to ignore them, or fail to acknowledge their significance, calendars still quietly mark the inexorable passage of time, day by day, precisely, and without deviation or ambiguity. They can gently remind us of lost opportunities, but more frequently they memorialize our milestones, commemorate our quests, and recognize the realization of our hopes and dreams. The simple measurement provided by calendars of the passage of time allows us to more easily recognize and to live in the here-and-now, while providing us with a regularly recurring and refreshing perspective that is a key to our continued growth and development.

Perhaps, if we are fortunate, a special calendar that takes the form of a book such as this one will increase our dedication and our commitment to Gospel principles. If it is used as the primer that it was intended to be, and we more comfortably think about the Savior and His Gospel, it might become just the tool we need to more earnestly internalize a working understanding of the Plan of Salvation. It might help us to realize personal outcomes that are consistent with God's foreknowledge of our potential. What better way, then, to create structure, balance, and eternal perspective, and to move in the direction of our dreams, than to think about the Savor on a daily basis.

Introduction

When "the Pharisees were gathered together, Jesus asked them, Saying, What think ye of Christ? Whose son is he?" Sadly, their sluggish response, "The Son of David," was tendered with little feeling or emotion. (Matthew 22:41-42). Although it was technically correct, it lacked spiritual horsepower. Its dearth of traction was obvious, its inability to generate spontaneity was palpable, its lack of energy to engage enthusiasm was noticeable, its incapacity to spark vitality was evident, and its failure to candidly acknowledge the powerful relationship that can exist between man and God was clear. Following the Savior's rebuke of their hesitancy and equivocation, none of the Pharisees were thereafter "able to answer him a word, neither durst any man from that day forth ask him any more questions." (Matthew 24:46). They had been weighed in the balances and had been found wanting, for they were spiritually bankrupt on an institutional scale. (See Daniel 5:27).

And yet, with adequate preparation, thinking about Christ could have generated the energy to lift them heavenward on a groundswell of emotion. This book will have fulfilled its purpose if it can elevate the worship of its readers to something more dynamic than the simple mechanical observance of a multiplicity of ceremonial rules, and if it can thereby help them to avoid the pit into which the Pharisees fell. Thinking about the Savior should be more than a repetitive exercise to be performed only by the numbers. As the daily antidote to our tendency toward pride, selfishness, and self-reliance, it should help us to catalyze feeling, capture emotion, contour attitude, crystallize thought, congeal passion, compartmentalize action, and convey sentiments that lead to our spiritual revitalization.

Since those were, perhaps, among the most important and penetrating questions that could have been asked of anyone, at any time in history, or at any place on earth, we can be sure that the Pharisees were not the Savior's only intended respondents. He cast a much wider net. The Master, Who expounded all scripture in one, demands that you and I answer, as well, that we might also have the opportunity to squirm under the microscope of His scrutiny.

It matters little whether we identify with the Pharisees or the Sadducees, with Buddha, Confucius, Guru Nanak, Zoroaster, or with gods of wood and stone. We may concur with the monotheism of Islam or the Bahá'i, the pantheistic theology of Hinduism, Shintoism, or Taoism, with secular humanism or irreligion, with Catholicism or Eastern Orthodoxy, with evangelicals, fundamentalists, or Protestants, or with the existential nihilism of the postmodern world. Paul observed of the Athenians, who were not so very different from us, that they were inclined to bow down before unknown gods, whom therefore they ignorantly worshipped. It is in the hope that this book will help you to stand independently in your witness of the true and living God, that "him declare I unto you." (Acts 17:23, see 1 Thessalonians 1:9).

You may be a trusting Timothy or a doubting Thomas, a spiritual giant or a philosophical naturalist, of a ready wit or resoundingly dull, earnestly enlightened or frivolously facetious, casually indifferent or energetically enthusiastic, a dedicated disciple or a distracted detractor, a true believer, an agnostic, or an atheist. In a moment of despair, you may have thrown up defensive dross designed to disregard, deflect, discourage, or disparage the question: "What think ye of Christ?" If you have wandered into disbelief, you may have deferred or deterred your response to: "Whose son is he?" If that day has already come, or if it looms large on your horizon, you can be sure that your stammering apologies will be unceremoniously swept aside when your true feelings are finally revealed.

In every case, no matter that you are a defender of the faith or an ambassador of the adversary, all of heaven will hold its collective breath as time stands still and your fate hangs in the air as a dandelion seed caught in the doldrums of a hot summer afternoon. How you answer will define you or destroy you, for your response will delineate your dreams, as it describes your destiny and determines how, where, and with whom you will spend eternity. I hope this book can help you to prepare for that great and dreadful day when you will be asked to stand and give your sworn deposition before God, angels, and witnesses, to be counted among the sheep or the goats, on His right hand or His left hand.

To insure that your answers might be animated with energy, to have no regrets, and to avoid the fate of the Pharisees, you have been given the Light of Christ. It proceeds from His throne as a powerful influence for good that is intended to groom you to receive the Holy Ghost. It is a gift that miraculously multiplies even as it divides within a universe populated with individuals whose actions are governed by free will. It is given, the Lord revealed, "that every man may act in doctrine and principle pertaining to futurity, according to the moral agency which I have given unto him." (D&C 101:78, see D&C 93:31).

It has been benevolently bestowed upon all of us by One Whom we can be sure "denieth none that come unto him, black and white, bond and free, male and female; and he remembereth the heathen; and all are alike unto (him), both Jew and Gentile." (2 Nephi 26:33). The Light of Christ stimulates our soul-sweat as it works on our conscience, our sense of duty, and our scruples. It provides a shield of protection against the corrosive spatter of perspiration cast off by the destroyer, who is insidiously and persistently working overtime to damage our doctrinal defenses, dull our spiritual sensitivities, diminish our charitable capacity, deplete our bountiful reservoirs of sympathy, and destroy our devotions, even as we labor with an equal but opposite intensity to deify our work on the earth.

The Light of Christ exerts a nurturing influence, as well. Although we must daily travel farther from the East, we are nevertheless oriented toward the radiant glow emanating from that distant horizon. It provides us with the regularly recurring reassurance of a religious recalibration that autocorrects with fortuitous frequency and celestial precision. It envelops us in an intuitive appreciation of where we came from, why we are here, and where we are going. As in a heavenly language that is rhythmical, melodious, soothing to our ears, and calming to our souls, when we hear the Spirit quietly whisper: "You're a stranger here," we are struck by the realization that we have "wandered from a more exalted sphere." (Eliza R. Snow). The Light of Christ examines what it means to be anxiously engaged, inspires us to plumb the depths of our commitment to the Savior, sensitizes us to the nobility of His work, expands upon the visions of immortality, and makes us more acutely aware of His glory, as it brings eternal life within our purview.

In a way, this book is a primer on midwifery, because one of its purposes is to facilitate the arduous process of our spiritual rebirth, by contributing to our preparation to answer with conviction the questions that were first posed to the Pharisees so long ago: "What think ye of Christ?" and "Whose son is he?" When we feel the urge to push His agenda, the Light of Christ can be our labor coach, providing us with just the right amount of encouragement to successfully deliver our witness of the Savior without being overbearing.

One exciting element of the manifestation of the Light of Christ is the constant stream of inspiration and revelation that cascades down from above. This insures that all may walk along illuminated pathways, and that no individual or institution may legitimately claim or have a monopoly on divine guidance. It exerts a leveling influence that is the great equalizer, giving each of us the same privileges to use our faculties of mind, intellect, and spirit to our best advantage, that we might discern between truth and error, no matter upon what spiritual plateau we might be currently relaxing. It permits us to listen with sensitivity and to be receptive to the cries of the downtrodden and oppressed, to see with a lucidity that allows us to be responsive to our environment, and to be benevolently blind to the shortcomings of others.

The Light of Christ provides us with a nurturing influence that makes it easier to have lips that have learned to articulate only positive expressions of speech and never speak guile, shoulders that have developed the strength to bear the burdens of those who have been battered and bruised by the vicissitudes of life and who may be faltering under the heavy weight of sorrow and sin, backs that have become sturdy enough to brace us against the fierce winds of adversity and the subtle wiles of the adversary, hearts that have become the receptacles of true and virtuous principles upon which we may draw in times of need, bowels that are moved to compassion for those who are struggling with misfortune, hands that have become accustomed to lifting those who are in need of support, and feet that have been conditioned to carry us to those who are imprisoned by poor choices, bad habits, or unfortunate circumstances.

Even now, heavenly messengers who minister by the Light of Christ are nursemaids to the nations of the earth, and use its power as a resource to reach out and caress those among them who are poor in spirit. Men and women of all persuasions feel that angels are watching over them. Witness countless newlyweds who are certain that their match was made in heaven before the world was. Others sense that they have been assisted by acts of providence, are the beneficiaries of divine intervention, have been touched by angels, are moved to compassion, or have been otherwise blessed to "walk in the light of the Lord." (Isaiah 2:5).

Guidance in the form of spiritual promptings and impressions are more common that many would suspect. Powerful intuitive communicators strongly influence nearly all of us to move in the direction of our dreams, toward a greater appreciation of the majesty and power of our Creator. Truly, He "is no respecter of persons" Who causes the sun to shine on the wicked, as well as on the just. (Acts 10:34). Therefore, we must venture forth out of the shadows, even beyond the direction we receive from the Light of Christ and the ministration of angels, if we want to begin to appreciate the special familiarity that the Lord enjoys with those whom He has characterized as "the children of light." (John 12:36). The more we think about Christ, the easier it is to craft with words the sensations that naturally flow to each of us as a result of the stirrings of those feelings of intimacy.

As I collected my thoughts in preparation for this endeavor, I realized how heavily I had borrowed from the towering examples of those who, over the years, have been my mystical mentors, my sensible chaperones, my spiritual guides, my surrogate saviors, as well as my compassionate critics. They are my avatars, who have shown me the way, strengthened my testimony, taught me humility, been there to steady and nurture me, applied the Balm of Gilead and bound up my wounds, provided both tangible and immaterial support, emboldened me with words of encouragement, and cheered me on with wise counsel. Even now, when I think of this multitude of angels thinly disguised as my family, friends, and peers, I remember the words of Sir Isaac Newton, who, when pressed to reveal the great secret behind his accomplishments, simply replied: "I stood on the shoulders of giants."

I have been privileged to do so, as well. As you think about our Savior while leafing through the pages of this book, you will notice that I have drawn upon the writings of William Tyndale, primarily from his excellent apology entitled: "The Obedience of a Christian Man." I have also quoted or paraphrased many of the General Authorities and lay members of The Church of Jesus Christ of Latter-day Saints, as well as numerous playwrights and poets, philosophers and humanitarians, authors, journalists, essayists, classicists, religious scholars of all persuasions, statesmen, sages, mystics, stoics, composers and lyricists. My friends and family, and particularly my wife Jan, have been more influential than they could ever imagine. I am fortunate to have been blessed with wonderful traveling companions during my journey. These gurus and guides have touched my life with a profound influence that has helped to shape the thoughts that I have clothed in words within the pages of this book.

In the end, however, I ask for your indulgence when you encounter the literal and figurative blemishes, the idiosyncratic foibles, and the objective and subjective imperfections that are sure to have worked their way into my expressions. I bear sole responsibility for them, and for whatever poetic license I may have taken if I have unwittingly fallen into the trap of adding needless ecclesiastical embroidery to foundation principles. Forgive me if, now and then in my writing, my passion has clouded my vision or overpowered my zealous intentions. If the syntax seems tortuous, if some of the daily entries seem too bland and others too spicy, if they are understated or have been given over to hyperbole, or even if, in their direction, they appear to drift over the line separating true doctrine from baseless speculation, leave them alone to simmer for a while before returning to sample anew their flavor. The reduction sauce of time may enhance the palatability of my perspective.

In any case, as the congealed distillate of my life experiences, my thoughts and feelings stand revealed as my innocent attempts to yoke my emotions to language. I hope that, at the very least, you find them refreshing, and will use them as food for thought, inasmuch as my viewpoint is sure to differ from yours, in nuance.

My dream is that we might feel the gentle caress of the hands of the Master Potter, as He turns our lives with the hand of time. I want Him to mold us and shape us as the Artisan of our destinies. "As the clay is in the potter's hand, so are ye in mine hand," said the Lord to His prophet. (Jeremiah 18:6). As Isaiah declared: "O Lord, thou art our father; we are the clay, and thou our potter; and we all are the workof thy hand." (Isaiah 64:8). The simple premise of this book is to encourage our thoughts to turn to the Savior, so that we may remain pliable and impressionable to the things of the Spirit.

All of us need to learn to utilize the divinely designed accouterments of the matchless and multi-talented Carpenter of Nazareth, Who will help us to construct the stages upon which will be enacted the drama of our lives. I can imagine that our efforts thereon will be validated by appreciative applause from the audience, and an occasional bouquet of red roses thrown at our feet. But it will be even more satisfying to remain as His poor understudies, and to give our best efforts to supporting roles in off-Broadway performances that count for more than mere entertainment.

His Plan does not require that we be the stars of the show. Our path of progress to perfection is a process, and not a point. We do not need top billing to fulfill our dreams. We do not seek to garner a People's Choice Award. Rather than becoming the objects of attention of an adoring paparazzi, I foresee us being enveloped instead in dazzling clouds of divinely directed diamond dust that glitters with thousands of points of light, and becoming the participants in daily dramas that far surpass the pomp and circumstance of any "American Idol" production. Ours will be performances exhibiting displays of celestial energy worthy of notice from above. As fire in the sky, the air in the theater of life will be charged with an electricity that represents the inevitable merger of the universal encouragement of the Light of Christ with the pointed and providential guidance provided by the Holy Ghost. When these influences streak in tandem across the heavens, their trajectories will coalesce to trace a flaming trail that sparkles over a vast cosmic ocean of thought. Over the ebb and flow of its tide, the Spirit will create an effectual bridge of understanding that is buttressed by the cohesive influence of the mighty foundation of faith.

My innermost longings to apprehend this vision are epitomized in this book. Some of the daily entries have been written as triumphant expressions of dreams fulfilled, while others reveal my efforts to fashion word portraits that depict my progression toward distant mileposts along the well-marked path that lies before me. But I suspect that many more define the past, present, and future challenges that are familiar to all of us. Our quest for the Holy Grail is defined as much by the obstacles we have encountered, as it is by the hurdles we have yet to face. We are molded by personal victories and by our commemoration of the achievement of our goals, but we are also refined by our frustrated plans, and shaped by our preparations to address challenges that lie just around the next bend in the road.

In the learning laboratory of life, experience is the active ingredient in a fertile matrix carefully created by God as He meticulously prepares the personalized petri dishes that are best suited to our individual circumstances. This rich culture medium becomes just the agar we need in order to nourish our metamorphosis, as we are transformed, not by maturation but by generation, into the full stature of our spirits. The infusion of a heavenly element readies us to receive with equanimity whatever might come during an incubation process that was designed to be just as challenging as it is rewarding.

All this leads back to the basic objective of this book, which is to keep the Savior in our thoughts, that we might encourage a daily atmosphere of reflection, maintain an eternal perspective, initiate positive change, and harmonize our behavior with His charitable example. My determination to do so has come, in part, thanks to Moroni, whose words have always stirred my soul as a voice whispering from out of the dust. On one occasion, he wrote: "I speak unto you as if ye were present, and yet ye are not. But behold, Jesus Christ hath shown you unto me, and I know your doing." (Mormon 8:35).

Because I will one day be asked to give an accountability report to the Savior, I try to heed King Benjamin's ancient but apropos warning to watch myself judiciously, to be the meticulous guardian of my thoughts, the scrupulous custodian of my words, and the prudent caretaker of my deeds, to fastidiously observe the commandments of God, and to continue evenly in the faith. (See Mosiah 4:30). As I hesitantly inch my way into the gathering twilight of the sunset years of my life, this admonition has invigorated me with renewed energy, and has instilled within me the desire to redouble my efforts, particularly as I have labored over the content of the book that is now in your hands, to make it not only objective, but also inspiring.

I have persisted because the simple questions: "What think ye of Christ?" and "Whose son is he?" should make a difference. These inquiries demand that we dig deeply within ourselves before we tender our responses, because it is all too easy to superficially retreat into colorless and insipid verbiage as the easy way out. If we casually and carelessly steer a course away from Him with offhand, dismissive, and inconsiderate comments, until He is conveniently out of sight and far from our minds, we can realistically expect in return no more than a stupor of thought. Any fleeting, albeit faux, feelings of liberation from the constraints of conscience will soon give way to an inner emptiness that cannot be satisfied with the poor imitations of the settled conviction in our minds of the peace that surpasses understanding, that could have been ours. If, in our knee-jerk reactions to the healthy opposition that stimulates our growth, we then kick against the pricks, we will surely further estrange ourselves from the Spirit, until we are left with neither root nor branch. We will be tossed to and fro by every wind of doctrine, as flotsam and jetsam on the sea of life.

None of us would choose to perish because of our willful neglect of the things that matter most, or to lead marginalized lives because we had intentionally become spiritually depleted on a personal or an institutional level. We persevere because we do not want to die of spiritual starvation, doctrinal dehydration, or intellectual inhibition, while only inches away from the living bread that would have satisfied our hunger, or from the healing fountains of truth that could have slaked our thirst. We elect to think about our Savior in positive and meaningful ways that lead us to green pastures and still waters. The process draws us into the warmth of His embrace, where we are permitted to enjoy an intimacy that allows us pause for a moment to feel the touch of His garment, before His strident call to action reawakens us to a sense of duty that quickens the pace of inexorable journey back to our beginnings.

Precious few "self-help" books address the issues of self-denial, meekness, and charity, or ask that we surrender to the greater good our desire for self-actualization, self-renewal, self-determination, self-fulfillment, or self-aggrandizement. Not often are we taught to concentrate our efforts on the quality of self-control that honors God's design, rather than some twisted temporal theory of emotional or spiritual well-being that lacks an upward thrust. But that is exactly what we must do, and that is what I have attempted to encourage in this book. We must "let go and let God." Only then, will we catch a religious fever that elevates our testimony temperature enough to get our juices flowing with an appreciation of Who He really is. Only then, will we experience the earth shaking and mind bending theophany that we are His spiritual offspring, and will we recognize the potential of our position. The precious emanation of familiar and soothing oscillations of energy resonating from within the limitless reserves that are selflessly shared by the Holy Ghost will carry us along on rolling waves of the spirit toward a more sure witness of the Savior's divinity. That is why we must keep Him in our thoughts.

This pulsing arpeggio ignites our souls with passion, and may have been the catalyzing influence that was missing from the pedantic model of righteous behavior that was adopted, almost by default, by the Pharisees. We want our preparation for the performance of our lives to include fast-scale runs through more than half a dozen octaves on all 88 of the glistening black and white ivory keys of experience. As we rehearse in our minds our witness that Christ is our Savior, we want to be accompanied by a celestial symphony that has been scored for every instrument. We want to expand our repertoire to include, not only inspiring artistic compositions representing every epoch of musical literature, but also our own original and signature harmonic inventions.

But most of all, in the orchestration of life, we want the Senior Recital that showcases our command of pitch, rhythm, dynamics, timbre, and texture, to be worthy of His approbation. Along the way, we want to find our way back to the Source of our inspiration, that we might one day enjoy master classes as we sit at the feet of the Maestro Who first created musicality by matching movement and form to the melody and mood of His celestial creations. We want to become reacquainted with our perfect fit. Then, when we have finally completed our dissertation on life, we hope that our composition may be recognized as our magnum opus. After we have successfully defended our thesis, we would like to be able to express our thanks at the exercises that not only celebrate our lives, but that also observe and honor our commencement. We hope to gratefully acknowledge our devotion to the one who became our doctoral advisor, who was none other than "the Christ, the son of the Living God." (Matthew 16:16).

We want to have a yearning to consecrate our lives to Him, and to throw ourselves upon an altar of faith that is of our own construction, whose foundation is buttressed by a supernal display of divine direction. We want to enjoy an unwavering confidence that drives us relentlessly forward so that we might one day squarely and unflinchingly meet His penetrating gaze with clear eyes, that His power to save might be unleashed in our behalf, that it might flow over our wounds as a healing balm.

When we look around, we want to find ourselves among those who have been Born Again, who are "called the children of Christ, his sons, and his daughters." (Mosiah 5:7). We want to experience the thrill of being spiritually begotten of Him, and of having our hearts changed through faith on His name. We want Him to be ever before us so that our thoughts might turn to Him without distraction, that we might feel His energy building within us until it lifts us to the zenith of experience where the lines distinguishing mortality from eternity blur, and we find ourselves consumed in a fire of everlasting burnings.

We want to be able to resoundingly declare that we have been born of God, and have received His image in our countenances; that we have experienced a mighty change in our hearts. (See Alma 5:14 & 26). Only then, through saving faith, will we be prepared to respond to the questions that loom before us: "What think ye of Christ?" and "Whose son is he?" As we ponder our relationship with the Savior, our proper prior preparation will prevent our poor performance. It will nudge us off our complacency plateaus, away from the trendy cafés situated along the broad avenues of Idumea, and transport us as on the wings of eagles beyond the boundaries of our self-imposed limitations, right to the edge of eternity, where "forever" will finally stand revealed before us.

At that moment, as the power fueling our actions charges our spiritual batteries and energizes our sight with infinite perspective, there will be created a pulsing stream of inspiration whose flow has no temporal or spatial boundary. We will be swept up by quickening currents into the direct experience of a holy communion with God. Although the heavens will always be higher than the earth, His thoughts will have somehow become our thoughts, and His ways our ways. (See Isaiah 55:8-9). We will be caught up in His work and His glory, and finally understand that "the universe is a machine for the making of gods." (Henri Bergson).

"Blessed are the poor in spirit who come unto me,
for theirs is the kingdom of heaven."
(Matthew 5:3).

January 1

As I think about my Savior,

I
weigh my
determination to
commit myself to focus
the full resources of my
energy on the observance
throughout the year
of my New Year's
resolutions.

For many
of us, the emphasis
just after the holidays is on
intangible resolutions – promises
to ourselves generally kept for a
few days or weeks, at best, before
they are summarily abandoned
and we return to our former
lifestyle. Instead, I will take
a lesson from the Apostles
whose ministry has been
recorded in their Acts,
rather than in their
resolutions.

January 2

As I think about my Savior,

I must
not allow my joyful
celebration commemorating
the New Year to succumb to the
excesses of selfish indulgence.

Gluttony
and drunkenness
prejudice the judgment of
the weak-willed. Fascination
with physical impairment blinds
us to the path of progress toward the
kingdom that is before our very eyes. Of
such individuals, Isaiah wrote: "They regard
not the work of the Lord, neither consider the
operation of his hands." (2 Nephi 15:12). They
are held captive because their character does
not harmonize with holiness. They are past
feeling, cannot commune with the Infinite,
and will never come to an understanding
of God as long as their overindulgence
demands an ever greater intensity
of validation for the same level
of gratification.

January 3

As I think about my Savior

and reflect upon
the holidays, I guard
against falling back
upon the world's
typical pattern
of giving only
lip service to
the story of
the Christ
Child.

In my
personal study
of the Bible, as I learn
more about Him, I remember
the caution penned by Sir Walter
Scott: "Within this awful volume lies
the mystery of mysteries. Happiest is he
of human race, to whom our God has given
grace, to read, to fear, to hope, to pray; to
lift the latch, and force the way. And
better had he ne'er been born,
who reads to doubt, or
reads to scorn."

January 4

As I think about my Savior,

and I slowly
decompress as I wind
down from the hectic pace of the
holidays, I hope to be sustained
by the spirit, so that when I go
to bed at night, I might
sleep in heavenly
peace.

"Blessed are the peacemakers, for
they shall be called the children of God."
(Matthew 5:9). They are the spiritually begotten
sons and daughters of Christ who go about actively
promoting goodwill. They are the fashioners of amity,
whose behavior models that of the Master, who was the
Prince of Peace. "Theirs is not the peace of this world, of
ease, of luxury, idleness, absence of turmoil and strife,
but the peace born of a righteous life, the peace that
lifts the soul, that day by day brings us closer to
the home of Eternal Peace, the dwelling place
of our Father." (J. Reuben Clark, Jr.). Theirs
is the peace that surpasses understanding,
the peace that comes from obedience
to Gospel principles.

January 5

As I think about my Savior,

my tendency
to be cynical is
overcome by my
capacity for
charity.

For over
two thousand
years, our celebration
of the birth of Jesus Christ
has renewed the promise of
a God-centered earth that is "full
of the knowledge of the Lord, as the
waters cover the sea." (Isaiah 11:9). In
all that time, it has become abundantly
clear that "no form of government, no
level of material well-being, will save
us. We will be redeemed only when
towers fall and Jerusalem triumphs
over Babylon. Finally, what is at
stake is not only intelligence,
but feeling. We have to
change our hearts."
(Abba Eban).

January 6

As I think about my Savior,

I
free my
mind from
distraction as
I put away the
Christmas lights
of confusion, and I
remember the reason
for His birth.

His
Atonement
has permanently
eliminated the effects
of physical death, and has
blessed every child of God with
the opportunity to have the eternal
consequences of spiritual death erased
through repentance. It can literally save all
of us from becoming angels of the adversary.
It does this by bringing into operation the Law
of Mercy that mitigates the requirement
for the satisfaction of the first law,
or the Law of Justice.

January 7

As I think about my Savior,

I realize that all of our hopes and fears have been met in the crucible of one shining moment in time.

"Be still,
sad heart, and
cease repining. Behind
the clouds is the sun still
shining. Thy fate is the common
fate of all," and "into each life some
rain must fall. Some days must be dark and
and dreary." (Longfellow). There is already more
than enough to worry about without adding to my
burdens by fretting about the future. Worry is interest
on a debt that never comes due. There are, after all, only
three types of control in life. First, are those circumstances
over which I have direct control. Then are those things
over which I have indirect control, and finally those
over which I have no control. A key to my peace
of mind is to learn where to most profitably
direct my energies and resources. The
Gospel can give me the perspective
that I need, especially on
my worst days.

January 8

As I think about my Savior,

I wonder what
ever happened to the
avalanche of letters the postal
service received during
the holidays that were
simply addressed
to "Santa
Claus."

This
is the hopeful
correspondence that
has been sent by children,
asking for pointedly specific
presents. Following the holidays, no
one keeps track of the number of thank
you notes sent to Santa from the grateful
recipients of all those gifts. On the other hand,
my gratitude to Heavenly Father for the blessings
He has showered down on me kindles a little spark
of celestial fire that glows within my bosom, that
is sent across the vast reaches of the universe,
all the way into the eternities to brighten
His day, as it has mine.

January 9

As I think about my Savior,

my resolve is
strengthend to make
a New Year's resolution
that I can actually keep:
To be more diligent in
my repentance.

Contrasted
against the backdrop
of His marvelous light, my sins
bring me sorrow. I feel terrible about
them, because I sense that I am profoundly
filthy. I want to unload and abandon them, and
am almost obsessive-compulsive about the cleansing
of my soul. I am broken in heart and have the spirit of
contrition, and I am teachable because I have prepared to
receive the Spirit. At this level of introspective discovery, I
will be moved to join in my supplication with the disciples
who, on the Day of Pentecost, asked: "What shall we do?"
The simple answer was to "repent and be baptized…in
the name of Jesus Christ for the remission of sins."
(Acts 2:37-38). Only then may I receive the
Holy Ghost, to feel an inner peace that
surpasses understanding.

January 10

As I think about my Savior,

I am
exhilarated
that, again and
again throughout
the year, I can open
the spiritual gifts
with which He
has blessed
me.

God has
provided me with
an effective antidote to
an array of poisonous telestial
tendencies that, like tares, threaten
to choke out the expression of celestial
sureties. Ultimately, I cannot be saved by
rallying around noble principles. Rather, I
will only escape death and destruction if I
have the faith that is necessary to unwrap
the best spiritual gift of all, which has
been symbolized by the precious
redeeming blood of His
Only Begotten Son.

January 11

As I think about my Savior,

the Plan kicks
into high gear, as
I seize upon the way
it has provided for
me to see with the
eye of faith, that
I might always
walk in the
light.

Too often, my
vision seems to be obscured
by doubt and confusion, and I can
find no one to whom I can turn, for no
one seems to know what to believe. Tensions
rise, the pace of life becomes frantic, vulgarity is
common, and righteousness is not a popular goal.
What a blessing it is to realize there is a haven that
is a place of rest from the turmoil of the world. Life
does have a purpose and direction that is evident
to those who heed His admonition to "be still,
and know that I am God," not only around
the season of His birth, but also every
day throughout the year.

January 12

As I think about my Savior,

it is my
good fortune to
be reacquainted with
the greatest story
ever told.

Simply
relying upon third
person accounts of the
Lord's birth and subsequent
ministry are no longer sufficient.
"Why shouldn't we have a religion
by revelation to us, and not just the
history of theirs?" asked Ralph Waldo
Emerson. The Restoration invites all
to drink from the fountain of living
waters. When I acknowledge God's
concern for me, I more powerfully
understand that these currents
and many more are part of a
continual stream of divine
guidance enjoyed by all
those who belong to
His Church.

January 13

As I think about my Savior,

the individuality of snowflakes
reminds me that each of us
is a unique child of God.

It was
ordained by our
Father in Heaven long
before the world was, that you
fulfill the measure of your creation.
(See D&C 88:19). Three million differences
within the human genome that is comprised
of three billion nucleotide combinations distinguish
you from every other human being on the planet. What
you see when you look in the mirror, then, is the product
of His unimpeachable judgment. It is the spectacular result
of His thoughtful consideration of an infinite number of
possibilities before He finally settled upon the perfect
blend of permutations and combinations to create
something that could only be described as
truly unique, that all of heaven could
celebrate as "you." When God saw
what He had made, He declared
that it was not just good, but
that it was "very good."
(Genesis 1:31).

January 14

As I think about my Savior,

I dream of
awakening to
a soft blanket
of white that
has covered
the wintery
landscape.

I am
reminded of
the words of Isaiah,
who said: "Though your sins
be as scarlet, they shall be as white
as snow." (Isaiah 1:18). "Many people
seem to have the idea that the Judgment
will somehow involve weighing or balancing,
with their good deeds on one side of the scales
and their bad deeds on the other. This notion
is false. God cannot allow moral or ethical
imperfection in any degree whatsoever
to dwell in His presence. He cannot
tolerate sin with the least
degree of allowance."
(Steven Robinson).

January 15

As I think about my Savior

following a
festive holiday
season, my heart
is full, even though
my wallet may
be empty.

It seems that
whenever I focus on
telestial trinkets, the line that
separates my wants from my needs is
blurred, and I have difficulty recognizing
the differences between poverty and wealth. I
am so much more comfortable when I seek spiritual
gifts rather than the profane baubles and ornaments of
the world. I realize that poverty is having so many
clothes, I haven't got a thing to wear. It is eating
so well, I have to think about going on a diet. It
is being loaded down with toys at Christmas,
and then being bored silly because there's
nothing to do. It is never stopping to see
the beauty of the world and smell the
poinsettia, especially during the
holiday season of the year.

January 16

As I think about my Savior,

I
inventory in
my mind's eye
the carefully stored
decorations that are the
symbols of the season: lights,
ornaments, stars, bells, candy
canes, and gift wrapping.

In His ministry, the
Savior also frequently used
symbols. He talked of lost sheep,
mustard seeds, pearls of great price,
fig trees, olive branches, hens, chickens,
birds, flowers, and foxes, bread and water,
and bitter cups. He told Moses: "All things have
their likeness, and all things are created and made
to bear record of me." (Moses 6:63). In reality,
"earth is crammed with heaven, and every
common bush with fire of God. But
only those who see, take off their
shoes. The rest stand around
picking blackberries."
(E.B. Browning).

January 17

As I think about my Savior,

I
contrast a
cold wind of
winter that stings
my cheeks, with the
warmth that I
feel in my
heart.

The chill
in the air stands
in stark opposition to
my conviction that I am "as
a white hot spark struck off the
divine anvil of God." (B.H. Roberts).
These flashes of faith ignite the flame of
my resolve, as I develop the power to do
whatever is right, no matter what the
consequences may be. It is my hope
that the resulting refiner's fire will
spark the process of purification,
resulting in the eradication
of the slag from my
nature.

January 18

As I think about my Savior,

I add my
own testimony
to the unimpeachable
witness of John, who long
long ago declared: "To him
be glory and dominion for
ever and ever."
(Revelation 1:6).

The evidence and
memory of the Lord's ministry
could have just quietly faded away,
but as time passed and events unfolded,
there was instead "no greater drama in human
record than the sight of a few Christians, scorned
and oppressed by a succession of emperors, bearing
their trials with a fierce tenacity, multiplying quietly,
building order while their enemies generated chaos,
fighting the sword with the word, brutality with
hope, and at last defeating the strongest state
that history had known. Caesar and
Christ had met in the arena,
and Christ had won."
(Will Durant).

January 19

As I think about my Savior,

I
reflect on the
fact that in order to
combat the influence of
evil in the world, the very
powers of heaven have been
brought to bear upon the
battles that seem to
continually rage
in my heart.

Satan never
sleeps, and "death
stands at attention, obedient,
expectant, ready to serve, ready
to shear away the people en masse;
ready, if called on, to pulverize, without
hope of repair, what is left of civilization."
(Sir Winston Churchill). From time to
time, direct intervention by God
is necessary to counter Satan's
relentless frontal assault
on the order of
society.

January 20

As I think about my Savior,

I receive a confirmation that
one day very soon, Zion
will surely triumph
over Babylon.

Zion stands
for something,
while Babylon will
fall for anything. Zion
quietly rededicates herself
over altars in the temple, even
as Babylon heatedly argues over
tables in the tavern. Zion exists to be
taught; Babylon wants to be told. Zion
learns with her heart; Babylon with its
head. Zion is created through sacrifice;
Babylon through selfishness. Zion does
require risk, but the security of Babylon
is at the expense of its personal growth.
Zion is founded and is grounded on the
order of the priesthood. Babylon exists
in the chaos and confusion of politics.
Zion promises peace, while Babylon
can deliver nothing more than the
absence of armed conflict.

January 21

As I think about my Savior,

I can see the pulsing
energy of a multi-faceted
glitter of light on new-fallen
snow, and in the numberless
reflections of its uniquely
individual crystals.

We, too,
may reflect the
light in our lives. Of
her mission experience,
Sister Joanna Hudson wrote:
"I am learning that the only way I
can increase my strength is to give away
that which I have received. I have realized
that at the end of the days when I expend the
least amount of energy serving others, I am
the most tired, and it is on the days when
I have served my heart out that I feel
rejuvenated." Wearing herself
out in service to others,
Joanna became a
prism of the
Lord.

January 22

As I think about my Savior

I cherish the gold dust of time, those moments when either consecration or temptation may hold sway, when my spirit can be either intensely rewarded or profoundly disappointed.

"Someone
once said that time
is a predator that stalks
us all our lives. I prefer to think
of it as a companion that accompanies
us on the journey, reminding us to cherish
every moment." (Captain Jean Luc Picard).
I can give time, take time, find time, buy
time, and even make time. The precious
commodity of time allows me to make
regular deposits to my spiritual bank
account, so that when the occasion
arises, or when an emergency
withdrawal must be made,
adequate reserves will
be available to meet
even the most
pressing
need.

January 23

As I think about my Savior,

I express to Him my
thanks for the capacity He has
given me to move forward
with confidence on the
path of progress.

The Savior
has richly blessed me
with wonderful tools that are
sufficient to the task at hand when
dealing with the uncertainties of life.
In the light of His Gospel, I see things as
they really are, and the foundation created by
my choices confirms my decision to follow His
teachings. In "the Father of lights" there can be
"no variableness, neither shadow of turning."
(James 1:17). The bedrock of His revealed
word provides a more sure footing than
does the uncertain and precarious path
thru the world of everyday that is so
familiar to me, that is congested
with telestial traffic leading to
conceptual cul-de-sacs and
personality precipices.

January 24

As I think about my Savior,

I
see the
fulfillment of
prophecy, that
His government
is even now being
re-established
among the
nations.

"In
some respects,
it is easier to govern
a whole people than oneself.
Of one ancient political leader it
is candidly recorded: 'And he did
do justice unto the people, but not unto
himself because of his many whoredoms;
wherefore he was cut off from the presence
of the Lord.' (Ether 10:11.) It seems that
we can cater to mortal constituencies,
but lose the support of the one
Elector who matters" most.
(Neal Maxwell).

January 25

As I think about my Savior,

I
listen
for the
unshakable
confirmation
of my faith, as
the Spirit quietly
quietly testifies of
His divinity.

Without
my faith, I may have
knowledge but still lack the
power to bring about positive
change. Initially, the faithful believe
what they do not see, and the reward
of their faith is to see what they believe.
As I develop spiritual maturity "by doing
my duty, faith increases until it becomes
perfect knowledge." (Heber J. Grant).
When these qualities merge in one,
the universe itself is energized to
become one vast engine for
the making of gods.

January 26

As I think about my Savior,

I rejoice, and sing not only with my
voice, but also with my heart,
and with my spirit.

Someone
once facetiously
observed that they
regretted their inability
to preach the Gospel with
such power that it would result
in mob violence. The point is, that
in the Last Days, discipleship must be
lived in crescendo, for the polarity resulting
when the Gospel standard is measured against
the shifting sands of secularism will only highlight
the behavior of those who are true to their covenants.
Standing out, as they do, members of the community
of Christ may sometimes find themselves in the cross
hairs of those who are intimidated by their shining
example. When the wicked have been decisively
engaged by the Spirit in an open dialogue, we
can expect them to assume a defensive
posture, but we must also be ready if
they go-for-broke by mounting a
desperate counter-offensive.

January 27

As I think about my Savior,

the
exercise itself
provides me with a
welcome break from
the "pressing" concerns
that would otherwise
clamor for my
attention.

I would hope
that my expanding
awareness as well as my
developing spiritual maturity
might allow me to follow general
principles and scriptural guidelines,
listen to the promptings of the Spirit,
and ask: "Are my actions holy and of
service to God? Am I doing good?
Am I using my agency to keep
myself unspotted from the
world? In my work, am I
honoring the Lord as
one of His true
disciples?

January 28

As I think about my Savior,

He speaks to my mind and to my heart,
as well as to my ears, with a power
that penetrates my rough exterior
and gives me the ability to
clearly "hear" His voice.

"I see the stars"
and can "hear the rolling
thunder, (His) power throughout
the universe displayed. Then sings
my soul, my Savior God, to thee, How
great thou art. How great thou art." (Carl
Gustav Boberg). In humility, I retreat from the
world, and for a defense set watchmen on my walls,
even as Babylon steadily advances beyond the borders of
propriety and misbehaves with abandon. My Savior steadies
my course as I navigate treacherous waters. I visualize my
destination, and know that He is the helmsman with the
necessary skill-set to guide me to that safe harbor. I am
enveloped within brilliant shafts of light streaming
down from above through broken clouds, and I
realize that they herald a glorious dawn that is
about to break for the children of promise
who are the people of His choice.

January 29

As I think about my Savior,

the witness that I receive of the
truth of His Gospel liberates
me from my bondage
to ignorance.

I can
almost feel
the hand of the
Lord, as He touches
me and bursts the fetters
of my mind to give me tools
sufficient to reach my dreams.
Once I have embarked upon that
path of progress, I know He will
bless me with a sense of purpose
and the moral responsibility to
provide assistance to others as
they embark upon a similar
journey. He will make me
more aware of my vested
interest in the eternal
welfare of every one
of my brothers
and sisters.

January 30

As I think about my Savior,

I remember that the earth "was once a garden place, with all her glories common, and men did live a holy race, and worship Jesus face to face, in Adam-ondi-Ahman." (W.W. Phelps).

Over and over
again, the swirling mists
of apostasy have benighted
the minds of men. When confusion
and controversy have arisen concerning
the simplest policies and procedures of the
Church, and when the doctrines of the Kingdom
have been compromised, it is because there could be
found no enlightened solution to the conundrum. The
ensuing and inevitable darkness could only be banished
by Heavenly Father and His Son Jesus Christ, Who have at
various times and in sundry places directly intervened in
our affairs in visions splendid. They have been on their
way attended by revelatory thunder and lightning
that is louder than the sound of rushing waters
and brighter than the sun at noonday, all with
the express purpose of illuminating our
minds with truth in a deafening
and dazzling crescendo.

January 31

As I think about my Savior,

the Spirit prompts me to
establish the unbreakable
bonds of friendship
with my fellow
travelers.

As His disciple, I
unhesitantly leave my
comfort zone to reach out to
others, and to figuratively and
literally clasp hands with them;
with my friends, family, neighbors,
and even strangers; to bring them into
the warmth of my faith and fellowship. I
am "set to be a light unto the world, and
to be the savior of men." (D&C 103:9).
I have been foreordained to make the
journey to the Lord only if I am in
the good company of those who
have come out of the world to
become fellow citizens with
me, and with the Saints,
in the household
of our God.

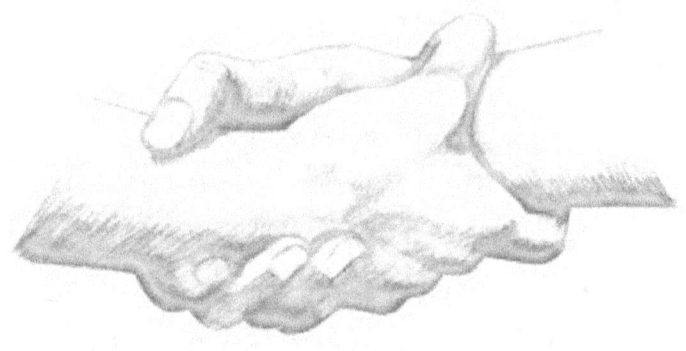

"Blessed are the poor in spirit who come unto me, for theirs is the kingdom of heaven."
(Matthew 5:3).

February 1

As I think about my Savior,

I am
optimistic
that, because
of the innocence
of children, peace
on earth might lie
within our reach,
after all.

Just as
soon as I have
become as a little
child, and I begin to be
meek, submissive, humble,
patient, and full of love, the
enticings of the Holy Ghost
will help me to put off my
natural tendencies to get
gain. As I recalibrate my
vision, through innocent
eyes I will be able to see
the cleansing power
of the atonement
of Christ.

February 2

As I think about my Savior,

my stewardship
responsibilities weigh
upon me even more
heavily.

I
have
tried to be a
good steward and
a faithful servant, to
be long-suffering and
able to endure to the end
in righteousness, for I know
that Babylon charges usurious
interest and has a reputation for
mercilessly calling its notes. When
I stand with Zion, I know that I will
discover within myself the strength
that is necessary to consecrate all
of my resources to the service of
God, in order to counter the
reckless efforts of Babylon
to plunder the land and
squander the bounty
of the earth.

February 3

As I think about my Savior,

I am encouraged by the power of the Gospel to awaken innate yearnings within the hearts of the children of men.

When men and women cannot control their appetites, "their passions forge their fetters." (Edmund Burke). The very moment they have made a compact with the devil, all tendered offers from above are summarily withdrawn, the gavel goes down hard, and their birthright is sold for a mess of pottage to him who is always the lowest bidder. The mission of the Savior was to break the bands of death and have the auction of our souls moved to Christie's. As Tom Paine observed: "What we obtain too cheap, we esteem too lightly. It is dearness only that gives every thing its value. Heaven knows how to put a proper price upon its goods." Though there may still be almost universal commotion from ocean to ocean, the quiet events that transpired in a grove that has since been called sacred have given us the tools to correctly value celestial goods.

February 4

As I think about my Savior,

and get a grip on
my senses, I come to the
sobering realization that
much of what I have
done in this life
has been for
myself.

However,
at the same time,
I understand that God
"overcame us with kindness and
to make us to do of love that very thing
which the law compels us to do. For love only
and to do service unto our neighbors is the fulfilling
of the law in the sight of God." (William Tyndale). As
I allow my altruistic sensitivities to predominate, I will
labor in behalf of others and begin to lose myself in
service. Then, when I really catch the vision by
acquiring an eternal perspective, I will give
myself to Him, even yielding my agency
to Him, because I have developed
implicit trust in His wisdom
and in His grace.

February 5

As I think about my Savior,

I see that "repentance goeth before faith, and prepareth the way to Him and to the promises. For He cometh not but to them that see their sins in the law, and repent."
(William Tyndale).

The greatest blessing that I could receive because of my recurring repentance is the opportunity to know that I am clean in the sight of my Father in Heaven, so that I can move along on my personal pathway to perfection. After my forgiveness because of the intercession of my Mediator, God will remember my sins no more. It is true that I might recall them, but only insofar as they serve a useful purpose to strengthen my testimony and help to mold me into a more stalwart and true soldier in the army of Christ. But culpability will no longer wear me down. Instead, virtue will enable me to sense the nurturing influence of the Holy Ghost, and to act upon those sweet and sacred feelings.

February 6

As I think about my Savior,

I am more
vocal, valiant, vital,
vivacious, vehement,
venturing, and vigorous in
my dogged, determined, and
durable defense of His divinity.

He
weighs in
on one side of the
scale, and the counterfeit
coin of Satan's spurious currency
clatters down in a cacophony of confusion
on the other side of the scale. My destiny hangs
in the balance, and ultimately, on every issue there
are three votes cast. I can be certain that Heavenly
Father will vote in favor of me, and that Satan
will always vote against me. It is I who must
cast the deciding vote, while all eternity
holds its collective breath as it counts
the ballots and awaits the outcome,
to see whether or not my calling
and election has really
been made sure.

February 7

As I think about my Savior,

I am
blessed to be
able to see what I
believe, through
the workings
of the Holy
Spirit.

As
my faith
intensifies, the
Lord's glory will rest
upon me. The doctrine of
His priesthood will be revealed
in marvelous simplicity and plainness,
and the Holy Ghost will purge the stain of
sin from my penitent heart, and it will reveal all
things. I will enjoy an endowment of power, as
angels watch over me, guide me, and protect
me. The kingdom will roll forth, even as the
walls of Babylon crumble and fall. Oases of
living water will spring up in the desert,
and I will slake my thirst as I kneel
before their life sustaining pools.

February 8

As I think about my Savior,

it is my
conviction that
dark clouds of error
will be dispelled as they
evaporate before the brilliant
rays of divine intervention
that are distinguishing
characteristics, even
the hallmarks, of
the restoration
of truth.

I will not be
ashamed to "declare
his doing among the people."
Without embarrassment, it will
be easy to "make mention that His
name is exalted." (2 Nephi 22:4). I can
then join with my fellow Saints who
have chosen to "stand as witnesses
of God at all times and in all
things, and in all places…
even until death."
(Mosiah 18:9).

February 9

As I think about my Savior,

in my heart, I reaffirm
my allegiance to
His name.

There is, in the
world, a fundamental
instability that is related to
hypocrisy, and those who weave
back and forth across what they fail to
perceive as the line between right and wrong
will pay an exorbitant price for their indiscretions.
They face a conundrum of cosmic proportion. Agency,
along with the inevitability of related consequences, was
envisioned to be the crown jewel of mortality, in order to
address the impasse created by opposition in all things. At
every fork in the road I must choose one way or the other.
I am free to follow one lifestyle or another, but not both.
That desire runs counter to the laws of nature, and so it
is fatally flawed. If, by choice, every now and then, I
renounce righteousness and pursue the rocky path
of disobedience, I am double-minded, and will
find myself traveling down a bumpy one-way
road that inexorably leads right up to the
slippery slope that lies above a
personality precipice.

February 10

As I think about my Savior,

I am struck with the
realization that I cannot
begin to imagine how
much He loves me.

It is
enough that "I
dreamed a dream in
times gone by, when hope
was high, and life was worth
living. I dreamed that love would
never die. I dreamed that God would be
forgiving." (Alain Boublil). If we learn to have
the pure love of Christ, if we have charity, then we
must be involved in the lives and fortunes of others
in ways that are equally intense and personal. As Jean
Valjean came to understand: "To love another person
is to see the face of God." (Victor Hugo, "Les Mis").
Even if it is at the cost of great personal sacrifice,
we need to find ways to reach out to our
brothers and sisters so that we may
enrich their lives, enhance their
fortunes, and calm their
troubled souls.

February 11

As I think about my Savior,

I muster the strength to endure,
and "to be blessed with Him in a little
tribulation, rather than to be cursed
perpetually with the world
for a little pleasure."
(William Tyndale).

As a
disciple,
I follow both
His admonition and
His example to turn the
other cheek, to go the second
mile, and I take up my cross to
follow Him to Calvary. This is not a
doctrine of passive resistance against the
forces of iniquity, but of active cooperation
with powers that are much greater than evil.
Now is the time for me to prepare for the
adversity that is a part of life, as well
as for the adversary who is sure to
harass me from the dark side. If
I am well prepared, I hope to
one day wear the laurel
crown of the victor.

February 12

As I think about my Savior,

I put
my temporal
"to do" list out
of my mind, and
turn my attention
to the weightier
matters of
the law.

What if I were to adopt
a list of virtues that adheres
to celestial standards? "Be grateful,"
urged Gordon B. Hinckley. "Be smart, be
clean, be true, be humble, and be prayerful."
That foundation would make it easier to focus on
what is really important. It would allow me to develop
a testimony that obedience to God is really my holy grail.
I would be provided with the motivation to work with all
my capacity to make it happen, whatever the cost. Then,
when the Lord had richly blessed me far beyond the
measure that I deserved, the price, that had once
been so painfully paid, would be recalled in
gladness, and I would receive full value
for my submission to His will.

February 13

As I think about my Savior,

I
listen
to quiet
whisperings
of the Spirit, and
although I may not
hear His coming, I will
nevertheless remain ready
to receive Him in meekness
and to welcome Him with
gladness into my
heart.

"I have
His promise
that all that He did
and suffered is a sacrifice, a
ransom, and a full satisfaction
for my sins; that God for His
sake will think no more on
them, if I have power to
repent and believe."
(William Tyndale).

February 14

As I think about my Savior

while studying the scriptures, I reverently review the relevant counsel and familiar stories I have come to love.

"These
words are
not of men nor
of man, but of me,
for it is my voice which
speaketh them unto you; for
they are given by my Spirit unto
you, and by my power you can read
them one to another; Wherefore you can
testify that you have heard my voice, and
know my words." (D&C 18:34-35). When we
"press forward with a steadfastness in Christ,
having a perfect brightness of hope, and a
love of God and of all men," we feast
upon His words and hear His voice.
Our experience is then validated
by the unimpeachable witness
of the spiritual confirmation
that we receive directly
from the Holy Ghost.
(2 Nephi 31:20).

February 15

As I think about my Savior,

He inspires me to
acknowledge the
inherent good
in others.

Christianity has
become the most universally
recognized religion in history, and
comprises a majority of the population
in 2/3 of the world's 196 countries. Almost
2 billion people, 31% of the world's citizens, are
members of 33,820 identifiable denominations. Islam
follows with 1.2 billion people. There are 14 million Jews.
(Source: "World Christian Encyclopedia"). The message of
the missionaries of The Church of Jesus Christ of Latter-day
Saints is not intended to detract from the devotion to correct
principles of any of the Christians or non-Christians among
whom they teach and testify. Those who are receptive to
the message of the Restoration are encouraged to keep
what the Spirit has already taught them to be true.
The purpose of proselytizing efforts is only that
"faith also might increase in the earth," and
that the Lord's "everlasting covenant
might be established."
(D&C 1:21-22).

February 16

As I think about my Savior,

the articles
of my faith become
the particles of my faith
that become inseparably
intertwined with my sinews,
and I commit them to action as
as well as to memory. As Gordon
B. Hinckley counseled, so will
I do: I will make a conscious
effort to remain grateful,
smart, clean, humble,
prayerful, and
true.

I hope to be
so deeply moved by
the virtue of the word
of the Son of God, that it
will become my perpetual
delight to be consumed by
His law, upon which I
will meditate both
day and night.

February 17

As I think about my Savior,

the
spirit illuminates
my mind, strengthens
my resolve, softens my
heart, and looses my
tongue, that I might
bear testimony of
His mission.

"Thou art an
holy people unto the Lord
thy God, and the Lord hath chosen
thee to be a peculiar people unto himself,
above all the nations that are upon the earth."
(Deuteronomy 14:2). In Hebrew, to be "peculiar"
connotes a special, covenant relationship. Hence,
Peter's characterization of the Saints as "a chosen
generation, a royal priesthood, an holy nation,
(and) a peculiar people." (1 Peter 2:9). We
wear with honor the emblems of our
covenant relationship with the
Lord, and we boldly testify
of His divinity to all
the world.

February 18

As I think about my Savior,

I resolve to embrace a
lifestyle that finds
favor with my
Father.

If I seem to take
pleasure in sin, it may
simply be because my level of
understanding harmonizes with
worldly standards. As long as I can
shut out the light of Christ, I may enjoy
the illusion. But ultimately, the discrepancy
between my deeds and Gospel ideals will
be so great that the short-lived pleasure
of my worldly ways will be devastated
by the realization that my experiences
were counterfeit. Wickedness, as it
turns out, never was happiness.
Ultimately, if I allow Satan to
be my master, I will come to
know that he was a liar
from the beginning,
who is unable to
deliver on his
promises.

February 19

As I think about my Savior,

I receive a witness that "from the beginning of the world, He sent His true prophets and preachers of his word, to warn the people." (William Tyndale).

One of the greatest contributions of the Prophet Joseph Smith was to share with the world his knowledge of what is to come after death. He has not only clarified my own understanding of heaven, but he has also created desire in the hearts of millions to follow the path that leads home. What he did validated the promises that my struggles during mortality would be worth it, and that I would look back on my experiences with appreciation for the personal growth and development that have occurred because I have chosen to participate in the clinical trial known as His Great and Merciful Plan. (And I know from my experience so far, that I have definitely not been given a placebo!)

February 20

As I think about my Savior,

I realize
that He notices
me, even though
I am one of the
least in His
kingdom.

As
Alma
counseled his
son Helaman: "It is
as easy to give heed to the
word of Christ," our compass,
"which will point you to a straight
course to eternal bliss, as it was for our
fathers to give heed to this compass," the
Liahona, "which would point unto them a
straight course to the promised land. Do
not let us" then, "be slothful" or move
slowly "because of the easiness of
the way." Instead, as if our very
lives depended on it, we must
"look to God, and live!"
(Alma 37:44 & 46-47).

February 21

As I think about my Savior,

the Spirit testifies
that "God was present with
thee in thy mother's womb and
fashioned thee and breathed
new life into thee."
(William Tyndale).

I took my
first breaths in a
heavenly nursery as
the spirit child of Parents
with distinctive qualities and
characteristics, and was raised by
Them to spiritual maturity, until I could
progress no more in my first estate. Then,
miraculously, I was added upon. I left Their
presence to fulfill a mission in a foreign
land that was created specifically for
me. Even now, living far from my
native soil, I am still Their spirit
offspring, I continue to enjoy a
generous measure of their
divine nature, and I can
almost palpably feel
Their influence.

February 22

As I think about my Savior,

my uncertainty, doubt,
and confusion give
way to conviction,
confidence, and
clarity.

An
energetic
missionary who
intuitively retained the
memory of his former life, and
knew the purpose of his call, who
had caught the vision and had incredible
enthusiasm and an unflagging positive mental
attitude for the work of the Lord, was assigned by
his mission president to be senior companion to an
elder who had difficulty getting along with others and
who had a particularly negative outlook on life. After a
couple of weeks, the mission president called his dynamic
young elder and asked how things were going. "Great!" he
replied. "My companion and I have discovered that we
have something in common." "What's that?" asked
his surprised president. "Neither one of us has
ever been to Africa!" replied the elder.

February 23

As I think about my Savior,

my preoccupation
with "I" and "Mine" yields
to my concentration on
"Thee" and "Thine."

The better
angels of my
nature will bear
sway. Those who
stand in opposition
to the expression of my
inherent nobility, the proud
and the haughty, feel neither
loyalty nor love for anything or
anyone but themselves. They do
not enjoy the blessing of harmony
and certainly not the peace that is
the province of the meek. Instead,
the father of lies and of contention
perversely enjoys the unfolding
spectacle of the self-destruction
of those whose fortunes and
lives have been irrevocably
impaired by patterns of
self-indulgence.

February 24

As I think about my Savior,

I
quietly
receive an
affirmation from
the Spirit that my
life is moving
in the right
direction.

"Be still,
and know that I
am God," He declared.
(D&C 101:16). Following that
decisive confirmation comes the
admonition to see that I "serve Him
with all (my) heart, might, mind and
strength." (D&C 4:2). All that He asks
of me is that I focus my affections, my
will-power, my reasoning faculties,
and my physical and my spiritual
energy on His worship alone,
and not on telestial gods
of wood and stone.
(See Isaiah 37:19).

February 25

As I think about my Savior,

my
senses
of hearing,
sight, touch,
smell, and taste
are heightened,
but there is more,
as I receive a quiet
confirmation that
the Gospel is
true.

Joseph
Smith taught:
"This is good doctrine.
It tastes good. I can taste
the principles of eternal life,
and so can you. They are given
to me by the revelations of Jesus
Christ; and I know that when I tell
you these words of eternal life as
they are given to me, you taste
them, and I know you
believe them."

February 26

As I think about my Savior,

I resonate
with "realities on the
other side of the veil that
become so obvious that
they can be explained
in only one way."
(Neal Maxwell).

"When the
gossamer veil called
time is too much with us,
let us recall that, ere long, it
will be no more. Meanwhile, let
us make allowances for the rapidity
with which it seems to pass, especially
when we are happy. Jacob found it to
be so, for 'he served seven years for
Rachel, and they seemed unto him
but a few days, for the love he
had to her.' (Genesis 29:20).
On such a scale, each of
us has but a few days
left in mortality!"
(Neal Maxwell).

February 27

As I think about my Savior,

I am grateful that my life has been blessed with inspiring testimony from His prophets.

Joseph Smith, and his successors who have subsequently held in their fulness the keys of the holy priesthood, have borne testimony as special witnesses of the Lord Jesus, Who is the Son of God. These men are at one and the same time prophets, seers, and revelators. They speak prophetically when they teach the corpus of known truth; they are seers who see with spiritual eyes and who publish hidden truth; and they are revelators each time they bring to the world's attention new truth that has never before been made known to our Heavenly Father's children.

February 28

As I think about my Savior,

I am
comforted
to know that
in my times of
greatest need, both
earthly and heavenly
angels will not forsake
me, but will respond to
my entreaties for mercy.

It is precisely
because of His concern
for each of His children, that
God in Heaven has charged His
angels with the responsibility "to call
men unto repentance, and to fulfil and
to do the work of the covenants of the
Father, which he hath made unto the
children of men, to prepare the way
by declaring the word of Christ
unto the chosen vessels of the
Lord, that they may bear
testimony of him."
(Moroni 7:31).

February 29

As I think about my Savior,

and yield myself to the
stirrings of the Spirit,
I trust in what it
teaches me.

The
preparation
for my schooling in
mortality began in the
pre-earth existence, and
now, the progression of my
rediscovery involves religious
recognition, a re-cognition, or the
renewal, recollection, recapturing, or
reknowing, rekindling, revitalization,
rejuvenation, and restoration of both the
sum and the substance of my existence. If
I deny or inhibit that instinctive response,
I am accountable, and to no small degree,
I condemn myself, for I knew the Savior
before this life, here on earth I have
become reacquainted with Him,
and I will recognize Him as
my Elder Brother in the
eternities to come.

"Blessed are they that mourn,
for they shall be comforted."
(Matthew 5:4).

March 1

As I think about my Savior,

I resolve to be more than
a "Christian of Convenience,"
who lacks the fire within that is
required by the demands
of discipleship.

Buried so
deeply within the
hearts of unconfronted and
uncommitted individuals that
it is almost inaccessible to outside
influence, there is a perpetual battle
raging. It pits their desire to serve the
Lord against telestial tendencies that twist
their focus inward and distort their vision,
causing them to falter in their discipleship.
"Two ways always lie before us; one leading
to an ever lower plane, where are heard the
cries of despair and the curses of the poor;
and the other leading to the highlands of
the morning where are heard the glad
shouts of humanity, and where
honest effort is rewarded
with immortality."
(John P. Altgeld).

March 2

As I think about our Savior,

I
determine to join
the chorus of voices
lifted heavenward,
that in unison cry
"Hallelujah!"

When
we have
united with the
household of Jesus,
we become firebrands
of faith. As subjects in His
kingdom, we can generate the
power to overcome every obstacle
that has been thrown up in opposition
to the economy of heaven. When Satan has
been thus bound, we "shall build houses and
inhabit them, and…plant vineyards, and eat
the fruit of them." (Isaiah 65:21). Because
of our righteousness, not a soul shall
"hurt nor destroy in all thy holy
mountain, saith the Lord."
(Isaiah 65:25).

March 3

As I think about my Savior,

I reach out to those who are
equally deserving of the
promises that have
been made
to me.

As they marvel at the
examples of His unconditional
love, members of the Church also
extend the hand of fellowship to others,
regardless of their circumstances. Babylon,
however, squints at these sudden sunbursts
of spiritual sensitivity, and would rather wear
designer sunglasses purchased at an exorbitant
cost at shopping mall boutiques. At the same time,
the children of the Lord look in wonder upon glories
that are just waiting to be revealed to the worthy.
With an eye of faith, then, and with increased
illumination provided by the dazzling light
of truth, they are able to clearly see the
radiant pathway that invites them to
journey with confidence in the
direction of the fulfillment
of their dreams.

March 4

As I think about my Savior,

I am
anxiously,
eagerly, and
even stressfully,
engaged.

Stress is
okay, as long as I
recognize and wisely
manage the tension that is
a part of every-day living. I
should be anxiously engaged in
good causes, and do many things
of my own free will, thereby to bring
to pass much righteousness. The Lord
has given me the power to be an agent
unto myself with the means to deal with
the pressures of living, by converting the
energy of position or potential energy,
into the energy of motion or kinetic
energy. This will then carry me
along productive pathways
into channels of creative
expression.

March 5

As I think about my Savior,

and
His love
gently tugs at
my heartstrings,
I feel the resonant
chords of charity
harmonize with
my divine
center.

Because
charity is a Christ-like
virtue, and is the embodiment
of His love, "it endureth forever, and
whoso is found possessed of it at the last
day, it shall be well with him." (Moroni 7:47).
Encouragement to Christian service prepares
me to be like Him. Its gift has been bestowed
upon me by the generosity of His Spirit, to
prepare me for the day when I will find
myself on my knees before His throne,
completely overwhelmed, and
even consumed, by His all
encompassing love.

March 6

As I think about my Savior,

the rock solid
steadiness of His
apostles of old
comes to
mind.

I think of
those inspired men
who "brought forth the key of
the sweet promises, saying, repent,
and be baptized every one of you in the
name of Jesus Christ for the remission of sins,
and ye shall receive the gift of the Holy Ghost."
(William Tyndale). Many in the Church find it easy to
follow their counsel only so long as it takes them on to
broad boulevards with conveniently located rest stops,
and to brightly lighted world stages that are filled with
the appreciative applause and the laudatory comments
of supportive audiences. But placed in challenging
situations with no-one looking, when there have
been no preparatory fortifying experiences,
and there are precious few positive peer
pressures to sustain correct choices,
it is far easier to falter.

March 7

As I think about my Savior

and His teachings, I am
provided with insights into
the nurturing influence of
the spiritual roots of
my relationships
with others.

The
foundation for
my happiness is built
upon the unshakeable bond of
our spiritual interdependency. The
links thus forged emphasize the capacity
of the ordinances of the Gospel to concentrate
their power to unite families and make life sublime.
The Savior taught: Abundance is multiplied unto the
the Saints "through the manifestations of the Spirit."
(D&C 70:13). Our eternal objectives that relate to
family exaltation stay in focus for only as long
as we pay strict attention to the spiritual
guidelines that have been provided
by our Father in Heaven, that are
amply illustrated throughout
the scriptures.

March 8

As I think about my Savior,

presidents, principalities,
magistrates and powers
pale in comparison to
the government that
is led by the King
of Israel.

As
soon as I
have learned to
govern my life by the
principles of the priesthood,
I will begin to move forward on
the path leading to God's kingdom.
And then, when I finally stand before
Him to render an accounting, I will realize
that the Lord was always by my side during
every step of my journey. Satan, that great
detractor, was always in opposition. As
it turns out, mine was the deciding
vote. In that electrifying moment,
I will know the answer to the
question: "Did I make
it count?"

March 9

As I think about my Savior,

and I am invited to
seek His influence "and
partake of his goodness,"
I will remember that "He
denieth none that come
unto him…and all are
alike unto God."
(2 Nephi 26:33).

All who
come to worship the
Babe of Bethlehem share a
common bond. They are no longer
Jehovah's Witnesses, Catholics, Mormons,
Episcopalians, or Quakers, but are "Christians."
Those who bear His sacred name will "be found at
the right hand of God, for (they) shall know the
name by which (they) are called; for (they)
shall be called by the name of Christ."
(Mosiah 5:9). As the Savior said:
"My sheep hear my voice,
and I know them, and
they follow me."
(John 10:27).

March 10

As I think about my Savior

in the comfort of my own hearth
and home, I beware, lest I draw
hasty conclusions to my
own advantage.

"It's true! The crown
has made it clear. The climate
must be perfect all the year. A law
was made a distant moon ago here. July
and August cannot be too hot, and there's a
legal limit to the snow here in Camelot. The winter
is forbidden 'til December, and exits March the second
on the dot. By order, summer lingers through September
in Camelot. I know it sounds a bit bizarre, but in Camelot,
that's how conditions are. The rain may never fall 'til after
sundown. By eight, the morning fog must disappear. In
short, there could not be a more congenial spot for one
to engage in happily-ever-aftering, than in Camelot."
(Alan Jay Lerner). We do not live in Camelot, but
we must not complain, because we have it quite
easy. In fact, "if (we) were stronger, (we) might
be less tenderly treated. If (we) were braver,
(we) might be sent, with far less help, to
defend far more desperate posts in the
great battle." (C.S. Lewis).

March 11

As I think about my Savior,

I am moved
to engage in
meaningful
scripture
study.

Often, on the routes
that climbers take to the
summits of towering peaks, fixed
ropes have been placed to minimize
the risks involved. The mountaineers use
jumars, or ascenders, that are attached to the
rope. These permit the climbers to move upward
without ever having to "let go" of the rope. The iron
rod is similar to these fixed ropes, and the organization of
the Church is like the jumar. The analogy, however, breaks
down in one significant way. Whereas mountaineers follow
ropes that have often been placed in proximity to perilous
crevasses, the Iron Rod plots a course that is always a
safe distance from disaster. The Iron Rod will not
lead us into peril. There will always be a zone
of comfort between clearly marked paths
of righteousness and treacherous
precipices of destruction.

March 12

As I think about my Savior,

I renew my
acquaintance with
those key players from
the scriptures who
were specifically
raised up from
before their
birth.

"The Lord
hath called me
from the womb," wrote
Isaiah, "from the bowels of my
mother hath he made mention of my
name." (Isaiah 49:1). "Once or twice in a
thousand years, perhaps a dozen times since
mortal man became of dust a living soul, an event
of such transcendent import occurs that neither heaven
nor earth is ever thereafter the same. Once or twice in
a score of generations, the hand from heaven clasps
the hand on earth in perfect fellowship, the
divine drama unfolds, and the whole
course of mortal events changes."
(Bruce R. McConkie).

March 13

As I think about my Savior,

I
marvel at His
stellar example that
sparkles on even the
darkest of days. He is the
Star of Bethlehem, whose
irresistible light became "as
a beacon upon the top of
a mountain, and as an
ensign on an hill."
(Isaiah 30:17).

When
we pattern
our lives after
His, we are on a
solid footing. He told
the Saints in Zarahemla:
"Ye know the things that
ye must do in my church;
for the works which ye
have seen me do, that
shall ye also do."
(3 Nephi 27:21).

March 14

As I think about my Savior,

I am able to enjoy the
happiness that blesses
untroubled souls.

Even as I
confront withering
opposition, my election
to righteously exercise the
gift of agency seals my longing
to yield my heart to Him, to ponder
the consequences of Gethsemane, to travel
with Him to Calvary, and to enjoy the sweetly
redeeming power of His Atonement, which is the
keystone of the Plan of God. When I keep His laws,
I experience the "happiness which is prepared for the
saints." (2 Nephi 9:43). That expression of joy will surely
transcend all of my temporal insecurities and discomforts.
It is the manifestation of a higher power with a capacity to
neutralize my pitiable and pathetic passion for pleasure
that is its worldly alternative, and that always seems
to jostle for my undivided attention whenever I
allow my resolve to waver in the face of the
relentless assault on my virtue by
my undisciplined desires.

March 15

As I think about my Savior,

I am
comforted to
realize that I am
within the sphere of
His protection, beyond
the influence of diluted
doctrine that lacks the
power to transform
my life.

Insult is added
to injury when hypocrisy
is accompanied by humanized
and spiritually impotent creeds, when
people do not really believe, but are only
the professors of religions that do not have
the capacity to save. This is abominable in the
sight of God, because the right way of the Lord
has been perverted. Form without substance
would require me to build the foundation
of my faith on corrupted principles
that cannot provide me with
the support I will need at
the end of the day.

March 16

As I think about my Savior,

I will find that
He has always been
there to steady my
trembling hands
and shaking
knees.

I have the hope
"through the atonement
of Christ and the power of his
resurrection, to be raised up unto
life eternal, and this because of (my)
faith in him according to the promise."
(Moroni 7:41). This is not wishful thinking or
misguided trust in an assurance that cannot be
satisfied, nor is it a high stakes gamble based on a
statistical probability. It is the inevitable reward of
well-founded faith, the product of my discipline
to control my desires and emotions within the
bounds the Lord has set. It will be the natural
outcome that is to be expected when I have
acted upon my established priorities that
are synchronized with the principles
of the Gospel of Jesus Christ.

March 17

As I think about my Savior,

and remember His
love for little children, their
potential gives me hope that "by
small and simple things are great
things brought to pass," and
that the world itself may
thereby be changed.
(Alma 37:6).

In
Abraham
Lincoln, Carl
Sandburg described
a man who was "both steel
and velvet, who was hard as a
rock and soft as a drifting fog, who
held in his heart and mind the paradox
of terrible storm and peace unspeakable
and perfect." The Gospel has the capacity
to conquer our carnal nature and harness
the raging power that lies within us. It
shows us how we might become
submissive, as little children.

March 18

As I think about my Savior,

and am
moved to
softly place
my hand over
my heart, I can
feel in its steady
beat the pulsing
energy of His
magnificent
love.

We
learn in
The Book of
Mormon that
after the Savior's
ministry among the
Nephites, their love for
each other was so great that
they were the happiest people
of all those who had ever been
created by the hand of God.
(See 4 Nephi 1:15-16).

March 19

As I think about my Savior,

I am prompted to seek out the
sustaining support and
altruistic assistance of
His sympathetic
priesthood.

In a
transcendent
act of condescension
and of confidence, God
transfers authority to His
blameless servants with no
thought or purpose other than to
bless me. The only limiting factor in
His design is my variable and somewhat
unpredictable and capricious application of
agency. That is the loose cannon that begs the
question: To what extent will I permit those who
exercise the priesthood to use it to my benefit, that
He may bless me beyond my wildest dreams? For
it is with their guidance that I am shown what
I must do to work out my salvation "with
fear and trembling" before the Lord.
(Philippians 2:12).

March 20

As I think about my Savior,

my obedience is no longer
an inconvenience, but
becomes my quest.

When I
have reached that
epiphany, He will endow
me with His power, even as
undisciplined minds continue to
be easily swayed by the siren song so
seductively sent by Satan. Unprincipled
character crumbles in the face of telestial
temptations that are so tantalizing and yet
so traumatizing. The more society focuses on
the flavor of the day, the less prevalent is the
legitimate rule of priesthood authority. This
substitution of the sacred by the profane is
abominable in the sight of God. One of the
most difficult things for the unconverted
to understand is that when we are
diligent in our obedience, our
agency is released, that it
may enjoy its greatest
expression.

March 21

As I think about my Savior,

a panorama
unfolds within
my mind to reveal a
drama of celestial scale,
that has already shattered
every box-office
record.

Although I may
feel, at times, that I am
on center stage, I will always
find myself in a supporting role
to the real star of the show, Whose
name alone appears in bright lights on
the marquee. He is the prototypical example
of the reality that Heavenly Father desires that
His children reach the full stature of their spirits.
That is why He has orchestrated a drama with His
Son cast as its central character. In a distant day, it
is possible that my corruptible body will take on
incorruption, and become clean, pure, and full
of light. I will have the potential to become
even as He is, and, in a sense, to shed
my role as His poor understudy.

March 22

As I think about my Savior,

I cannot allow myself the luxury of a supposed interruption in my spiritual education, even in the anticipation of a "spring break" from my secular studies.

The
graduate
school of hard
knocks will teach
me what I learned in
spiritual kindergarten.
Any disappointments that I
may experience along the way
are, in reality, just speed bumps on
the strait and narrow path leading to
the Savior. These are designed to allow
me to ratchet down the hectic pace of my
life, so that I might be able to stop and smell
the roses, at least during weekly preparation
days that have been integrated into my mortal
curriculum. It is all part of the divine tutorial
training that has been programmed into my
mission, that I receive while I am on His
errand away from my heavenly home.

March 23

As I think about my Savior,

I become less preoccupied with the talking heads of
a media that wobbles with unsteadiness because
it no longer has both feet on the ground.

If individuals
seldom receive divine
tutoring, it is only because
they repeatedly look in all the
wrong places for inspiration. In
days past, the prophets continually
warned Israel against dalliances with
magicians, sorcerers, witches, familiar
spirits, astrologers, and exorcists, as well
as against participation in enchantments
and divinations. In our day, we are all
familiar with equivalent distractions
by those who wish to do harm to
others. Sometimes, the innocent
are led astray, and are kept
from discovering the truth
for themselves, simply
because they do not
know where to
find it.

March 24

As I think about my Savior,

and about one brief shining moment
in Judea over 2,000 years ago, the
breathtaking expanse of
eternity is unfolded
to my view.

In a not too
distant day, when
the veil has been removed
from my eyes, I will find that I
am awash in a greater comprehension
of the hidden spiritual world. More than just
with a glimmer of light, but with crystal clarity, I
will see the wide expanse of eternity from the time I
was uncreated intelligence, through my development
as a spirit child of my Heavenly Father, on to mortality,
and finally to my reunion with Him in the resurrection.
"Knowledge will rush in from all quarters. It will come
in like the light that flows from the sun, penetrating
every part, informing the Spirit, and giving understanding concerning ten thousand things at the
same time; and the mind will be capable
of receiving and retaining all."
(Orson Pratt).

March 25

As I think about my Savior,

I recall
the circumstances that
surrounded the Annunciation,
celebrated on March 25 of each
year, to the virgin Mary, that
she would conceive by the
power of the Holy Ghost
and become the mother
of the Son of God.
(Luke 1:30).

"Motherhood,"
declared David O.
McKay, "is the greatest
potential influence for good
in human life. A mother's image
is the first that stamps itself on the
unwritten pages of the young child's
mind. It is her caress that first awakens
a sense of security. Her tender kiss is the
first realization of affection, sympathy and
tenderness, the first real assurance that there
is love in the world. Motherhood is the
noblest calling in the world."

March 26

As I think about my Savior,

I resolve
to do as the King
James Translators of the Bible
encouraged, to be overcome with
the fire of God "every day at home,
by religious and learned discourse, by
frequenting the house of God, by hearing
the Word preached, by cherishing the
Teachers thereof, by caring for the
Church, as a most tender and
loving nursing Father"
would have us do.

When I am
thrilled with life,
I will be "enthusiastic,"
a term that is derived from a
root word that conveys the thought:
"God is with you," "Possessed by God,"
or "Celestial inspiration." Truly,
if I have lived to learn, and
have learned to love,
I'll love to live.

March 27

As I think about my Savior,

faith in the Atonement
gives substance to
my desire to
repent.

The Savior
was "born to raise
the sons of earth; born to
give them second birth." ("Hark,
The Herald Angels Sing"). When I
live in harmony with the principles of
the Gospel, I am in a dynamic state of
improvement that leads to perfection. I
am admonished to cherish virtue, and
to cling to the hope "that honesty and
integrity are central to our conduct,
that civility is to be practiced, that
kindness shown to others is our
responsibility, and that respect
for the beliefs and practices of
others cannot be avoided" if
we hope to be called by
His name. (Gordon
B. Hinckley).

March 28

As I think about my Savior,

I am humbled to "submit to
his nurture and chastening,
and not withdraw myself
from his correction."
(William Tyndale).

I am struck by the
realization that I am not
alone as I continue to endure
what feels very much like a painful
lack of recognition, humiliating rejection,
unwarranted discrimination, uncomfortable
adversity, unmerited disregard, undeserved
misfortune, and relentless opposition. It is so
difficult to put my trials and tribulations in
their proper perspective and to understand
that, no matter what my experiences may
be, no matter what curves life may throw
at me, they are just the normal growing
pains of mortality. In my mind, I try to
accept the gentle reassurance of Hans
Christian Anderson, who reminded
us that "each of our lives is a fairy
tale written by God's fingers."

March 29

As I think about my Savior,

I "tingle with the consciousness of
my kinship with the Infinite."
(David O. McKay).

The
power of the
Savior stems from
love, in contrast to the
transient and counterfeit
illusion of authority that is
only driven by greed, avarice,
lust, and an unrighteous desire for
dominion. It is not too difficult to see
Satan's fingerprints that are smeared all
over programs and pronouncements that are
promoted by parties that pander to provincial
policies. With perseverance and preoccupation,
he props up paltry, petty, and personal plans that
lack piety or a palpably proven priesthood purpose
or perspective, and he persistently persuades people
who are unprincipled, from whom all patience has
plummeted, to pursue perilous pathways that
can only lead to one inevitable outcome,
and that is punishment, pure
and simple!

March 30

As I think about my Savior,

His
Spirit
brings such
peace to my soul
that I am moved to
exclaim that all is calm
and bright in the
world.

It was the Master of the elements who commanded the sea to be still, and it instantly ceased its commotion. Then, in the ensuing calm, His companions "marvelled, saying, What manner of man is this, that even the winds and the sea obey him!" (Matthew 8:26). Of the Roman Empire, Cicero said: "He who controls the sea, controls everything," but his focus, in light of the Lord's stunning exercise of authority while upon the stormy Lake of Gennesaret, was clearly far too narrow.

March 31

As I think about my Savior,

I find myself twenty four
hours closer to Home.

Here you are, home
from your mission. Think of the
people you met, those you helped,
how you have grown both physically
and spiritually. There is mother, waiting
to embrace you, standing just a bit behind
father, who is clearly bursting with pride. Are
those tears of happiness on her cheeks? Father is
first to strike hands with you, before he hugs you
tenderly. Mother puts her arm around your waist,
and escorts you to the familiar surroundings of the
room that has been prepared for your homecoming.
The atmosphere is pungent with a heavenly aether
that is punctuated by the melodious strains of
your native language. Every detail is just as
you had imagined it would be, including
the reassuring radiant heat of a celestial
fire kindled beforehand by father. You
know this is just where you belong,
at home once again, with your
Heavenly Father and
Mother.

"Blessed are the meek,
for they shall inherit the earth."
(Matthew 5:5).

April 1

As I think about my Savior,

I have an
opportunity
to participate
in yet another
dress rehearsal
prior to His
millennial
reign.

In
light of
the limited
recognition of
the Restoration of
the Gospel during the
last 186 years, one must
wonder just how the Lord
Himself will be received at
His Second Coming, when
there will be many who
will ask: "What are
these wounds in
thine hands?"
(D&C 45:51).

April 2

As I think about my Savior,

I try to comprehend how He was able to organize the elements from out of the void, in order to create a universe that would become "a machine for the making of Gods."
(Henri Bergson).

In King Benjamin's revelatory address to the people of Zarahemla, he taught: "Because of the covenant which you have made, you shall be called the children of Christ, his sons, and his daughters; for behold, this day he hath spiritually begotten you; for you say that your hearts are changed through faith on his name; therefore, you are born of him." (Mosiah 5:7). I believe the promise of our Lord, that after their sojourn in mortality would "the righteous shine forth as the sun in the kingdom of their Father." (Matthew 13:43). In the end, when our only thought is to glorify God, our "bodies shall be filled with light," and we shall comprehend the solemnities of eternity.
(D&C 88:67).

April 3

As I think about my Savior,

it gives me joy
to realize that one
day, I shall meet
Him in the
skies.

I am a
joint-heir with
Christ when I enter
into covenants with my
Father in Heaven. Only then
are the bands of death broken,
and am I liberated from bondage
to sin. "There is no other name given
whereby salvation cometh," said Benjamin.
"Therefore, I would that ye should take upon
you the name of Christ, all you that have entered
into the covenant with God." (Mosiah 5:8). Is it any
wonder that The Church of Jesus Christ of Latter-day
Saints is missionary oriented, and that the Savior
has proclaimed that it "is the only true and
living church upon the face of the whole
earth, with which I, the Lord, am
well pleased?" (D&C 1:30).

April 4

As I think about my Savior,

I link my prayers
with those of the angels in
heaven, in the hope that the
time will be hastened when
every son and daughter of
God will honor Him,
and praise His
Holy name.

I pray for
a unity of the
faith, and a time
when all will worship
the Lord Jesus in plainness
and in truth. My understanding is
that the scriptures speak unmistakably
about our personal relationship with the
Son of God. As did Nephi, I emphasize that
"we talk of Christ, we rejoice in Christ, we preach
of Christ, we prophesy of Christ, and we write
according to our prophecies, that our children
may (confidently) know to what source they
may look for a remission of their
sins." (2 Nephi 25:26).

April 5

As I think about my Savior,

I concede
that His love
for me defies
measurement,
and is beyond
my ability to
understand.

Even as I reach
out to others with my
timid and hesitant efforts, my
love for God becomes one of my
fundamental virtues, as it expands my
capacity for courtesy, gentility, decency,
dignity, and consideration. On the treadmill
of life, when we regularly elevate our heart
rates with the exercise of charity, we are
blessed with the increased strength to
endure in righteousness. It is less
likely that our hearts will fail us
by becoming congested with
vulgarity, insensitivity,
crudity, incivility,
or ignobility.

April 6

As I think about my Savior,

the
spirit quietly
infuses me with
confidence that His
ministry will continue as
"long as time shall last, or
the earth shall stand, or
there shall be one man
upon the face thereof
(yet) to be saved."
(Moroni 7:36).

"Whosoever repenteth
and cometh unto me," said
the Lord, "the same is my church."
(D&C 10:67). Ever since the Restoration of
Gospel truth on April 6, 1830, His messengers
have taught this doctrine without modification.
The keystone of salvation is founded upon grace,
that will be extended to me if I but exercise
saving faith in His name and enter into
the strait and narrow path through
the clearly defined portal of
baptism by immersion.

April 7

As I think about my Savior,

His example reminds me of my covenant to be "bound to submit myself and serve my brethren, and to give myself for them, and to win them" to Him.
(William Tyndale).

"I sought my soul, but my soul I could not see. I sought my God, but my God eluded me. I sought my brother, and I found all three." (William Blake). Sometimes, the Lord sends His ablest missionaries to His most wicked children. He arms them well, with unwavering faith, a sure knowledge of Gospel principles, firm and abiding testimonies of the doctrines of the Kingdom, of the Plan of Salvation, and of the Lord Jesus, a spiritual endorsement by file leaders, the continual prayers that are offered to heaven by the congregations of the Saints, as well as an endowment of spiritual and priesthood power that is reserved for faithful patrons who come to worship in the temple of God.

April 8

As I think about my Savior,

I come
to a greater
appreciation
of the timeless
nature of God's
gift to the
world.

Through
the manifestations
of the Spirit, God has been
able to confound "the worldly
wise, enemies to the wisdom of God,
our deep and profound wells without water,
our clouds without moisture of rain, natural souls
without the Spirit of God." (William Tyndale). To
these hardened skeptics, there have been given
many signs in heaven. Their purpose has
been to provide additional witnesses
of the divinity of the Savior. When
the world finally comprehends
their significance, all shall
stand amazed, and
wonder.

April 9

As I think about my Savior,

I marvel that He is no
respecter of persons.
(See Acts 10:34).

The
admission
policy of heaven
is really quite simple,
is clearly articulated, and
is specific in its requirements
Those of any race, creed, color, or
national origin are welcome to live in
any of a number of the mansions within
their Father's extensive real estate holdings,
in a community that is gated, with Jesus Christ
guarding the way, provided that they maintain
ideals and standards that are in harmony with
those of the Church that bears His name, and
that they meet all of the other requirements
that have been, or may be, published in its
C.C.&R.s, including the following: Faith,
repentance, baptism, and the various
ordinances that are performed by
legal administrators who
hold the priesthood.

April 10

As I think about my Savior,

I reflect on the miracle that the story has been told over 2,000 times, without revision.

The
faithful of every
age and season have
preserved and passed on
the wonderful story, although
there have been many for whom it
has become dreamlike, a fairy tale that
attempts in futility to convey power and
knowledge without the help of continuing
revelation. Moroni saw that there would be
many in the Last Days who had "transfigured
the holy word of God," or who had changed its
appearance and substance. (Mormon 8:33). No
wonder that Another Testament of Jesus Christ
became necessary in order to confirm the faith
of a people who were familiar with the four
Gospels, but who were, at the same time,
in ignorance of additional knowledge
that would illuminate the truth,
and not just multiply mirrors
without increasing
the light.

April 11

As I think about my Savior,

I
embrace the
mind-expanding
possibility that, one day
in a far-distant future,
I might be like Him
Who is both my
Mentor and
Example.

He
offers me the
gifts and powers
by which I may attain
His stature and perfection,
so that I may enjoy not only what
He has, but also what He is. "If ye by
the grace of God are perfect in Christ,
and deny not his power, then are ye
sanctified in Christ by the grace of
God, through the shedding of the
blood of Christ, that ye become
holy, without spot."
(Moroni 10:33).

April 12

As I think about my Savior,

I am comforted by the reassurance that while repentance, reconciliation, and redemption might seem unreasonable to rational minds, they are eternal reference points to which I may relate.

The Savior taught that we should be perfect, even as He is perfect, for otherwise we cannot inherit the kingdom of God. (3 Nephi 12:48). Perhaps He meant that we can become as He is by being perfect in our repentance, so that we may become holy and without spot. After explaining the great Plan of Redemption to his people, which solved the dilemma created by God's demand for perfection coupled with our inability to lead sinless lives, the prophet Jacob simply stated: "O be wise; what can I say more?" (Jacob 6:12). Moroni essentially offered the same counsel, when he urged: "Be wise in the days of your probation: strip yourselves of all uncleanness. Ask with a firmness unshaken, that ye will yield to no temptation, but that ye will serve the true and living God." (Mormon 9:28).

April 13

As I think about my Savior,

the Spirit
gently encourages
me to find my comfort
zone, and then to probe its
borders, to engage in acts of
"Quiet Christianity."
(C.S. Lewis).

Often,
even without my
conscious recognition,
my gestures are prompted by
inspiration that leads me to those
in need, and so I am doubly blessed as
I simultaneously receive, even as I give. But
when I am "expecting the spectacular," I "may
not be fully alerted to the constant flow of revealed
communication" that comes. (Spencer W. Kimball).
In contrast to the marketing messages of Madison
Avenue that are pleasing to those with itching
ears and carnal natures, the whisperings of
the Spirit strike the more sensitive and
selective chords of the few who
are the elect of God.

April 14

As I think about my Savior,

I soberly remember that "to
be great in the kingdom of
God, is to do service, and
take pain for others."
(William Tyndale).

None of
us would be
surprised to read in
the scriptures that to be
righteous is not to turn your
face "to the East or to the West,
but righteousness is this: Whosoever
believeth in God, and the Last Day and
in angels, and the Book and the Prophets,
and whosoever, for the love of God, giveth
of his wealth unto his kindred, unto orphans,
and the poor, and the wayfarer, and the beggar,
and for the release of captives; and who observeth
prayer, and when they have covenanted, fulfill their
covenant; and who are patient in adversity and
hardship, and in the time of violence; these
are the righteous; these are they
who believe in the Lord."
(Koran, ii:177).

April 15

As I think about my Savior,

I see
in His birth
subtle hints of
my own divinity,
for I know that I
have come from
God trailing
clouds of
glory.

Recurring
repentance releases
me from the bondage of
sin, unleashes the powers of
heaven in my behalf, and qualifies
me by worthiness to enjoy the blessings
reserved for the faithful. The Atonement of
Christ makes it possible for me to overcome my
limitations and to position myself to reach my
potential. As I live the Celestial Law of the
Lord, I can feel the commencement of my
spiritual transformation, as I begin
to fulfill my destiny as
a child of God.

April 16

As I think about my Savior,

and
confess
my sins. His
compassion and
His forgiveness
overcome me.

With
the exercise of
the great and terrible
principle of moral agency,
two conditions immediately
become obvious: The opportunity
to make choices in an atmosphere of
opposition, and the necessity of facing the
consequences that are related to those choices.
The urgency of reconciliation to the laws of heaven
through atonement is less apparent, but is even more
important. By the mouth of His prophet, the Lord
has warned: "I have spoken it, I will also bring
it to pass; I have purposed it, I will also do it.
Hearken unto me, ye stouthearted, that
are far from righteousness."
(Isaiah 46:11).

April 17

As I think about my Savior,

my familiarity
with the details of His
mortal ministry enlarges
my appreciation of
the Great Plan of
Happiness.

This
awareness helps
to explain the growth
rings of various widths that
define my sojourn on earth, puts
in proper perspective my trials and
tribulations, answers the questions that
have troubled my spirit, and enables me
to comprehend the solemnities of eternity
with greater clarity. As my understanding
expands, I am permitted to see with the
penetrating eye of faith, and the sum
of that experience establishes a sure
foundation upon the bedrock
of unchanging principles
that I recognize as
His Gospel.

April 18

As I think about my Savior,

The Spirit assuages my insensitivity, as a deep tissue therapist would massage stiffness or inflexibility in muscles.

The
Restoration
allows me to do
more than "multiply
mirrors and study angles
without increasing the light."
(B.H. Roberts). The Church stands
as an independent witness of the Lord,
and it is outward evidence of the restoration
of the truth following a long night of apostasy.
Before joining the Church, I stood on neutral
ground. Having made a covenant with the
Lord, however, I can never again have it
both ways. Those who are members of
The Church of Jesus Christ of Latter-
day Saints become His willing
ambassadors, ready to stand
and bear testimony at all
times, and in all
places.

April 19

As I think about my Savior,

I see
Him as
the Chosen
One who was
foreordained from
before the foundation
of the world to be
my Savior.

Our Lord
was the firstborn of
all of the spirit children of
our Heavenly Father, and the
greatest of all, Who understood the
Plan of Salvation, Who by His example
had already prostrated Himself upon the
altar of sacrifice for His pre-mortal family.
As God declared to His offspring who were
gathered together at the council: "Behold my
Beloved Son, which was my Beloved and
Chosen from the beginning, (Who) said
unto me: Father, thy will be done,
and the glory be thine forever."
(Moses 4:2).

April 20

As I think about my Savior

and His influence, I take
comfort in the hope that
peace and good will
toward men really
do have a chance
of becoming
realities.

As I
look all around at
a world that is in turmoil,
like a train wreck in slow motion,
the Gospel of Jesus Christ provides a
refuge from the uncertainties of life, and the
Church remains an island in the storm. To those
who are unsure, tentative, and hesitant, it speaks
a language of stability, direction, and of purpose.
My recognition and understanding of spiritual
promptings, and my capacity to act upon
them, is only possible because He has
provided me with "the key of the
mysteries of the kingdom, even
the key of the knowledge of
God." (D&C 84:19).

April 21

As I think about my Savior,

I try to be more
grateful that His word
is tendered without
money or price.

Too
often, I look
a gift horse in the
mouth, finding fault
with that which has been
freely proffered. To plumb the
depths of the treasury of the Lord's
Atonement, it is only necessary for me
to pay the price of a broken heart and a
contrite spirit. He provides me with counsel
in supportive scriptures that contain a wealth
of doctrine imbedded in a historical matrix that
touches on my personal experience in a thousand
different ways. These presage every anticipated
and unforeseen obstacle to my progression, in
order to make me more comfortable during
what could be perceived as an arduous
journey in the direction of my
heavenly home.

April 22

As I think about my Savior,

I try to envision what life
must be like in Zion.

I adopt the
invigorating lifestyle
of Zion, in contrast to the
subsistence level of existence
that is so characteristic of Babylon's
routine. I emulate Zion's listening ear,
even as Babylon speaks in a confusion of
tongues. I have learned to appreciate Zion's
firm grip on reality, as Babylon grasps at straws
in a confusion that is begotten by an illusion of its
own making. I admire Zion's steady dedication to
spiritual absolutes, but I pity Babylon's vacillation
while she tosses to and fro in the vacuum of moral
and spiritual relativism. I have witnessed the focus
of Zion, as well as Babylon's congenital spiritual
short-sightedness. I am comforted that Zion is
grounded on a bedrock of foundation truth,
whereas Babylon basks in a false sense of
security, confuses values for principles,
and proclaims the unsupportable
lie that "all is well in Zion."
(2 Nephi 28:21).

April 23

As I think about my Savior,

patterns of reflection are imprinted upon my soul, tracing a pathway to my potential, and breaching the barriers of my self-imposed limitations.

Whenever I allow my priorities to fall into disarray, the power to bring about positive change slips between my fingers, and I lose my sense of purpose. But then, as soon as I have reacquired my fix on the Lord, Who is my Polaris, the clarity of my vision once again reveals my untapped potential. With lucidity that feels like a breath of fresh air on my cheek after a summer storm, I discover within myself the reservoirs of energy that allow me to pursue principles of perfection that are reflected by His example and that have been powerfully validated by the Spirit. I am invested to heed Paul's counsel. He urged: "Those "things which ye have…learned, and received, and heard, and seen in me, do." (Philippians 4:9).

April 24

As I think about my Savior,

and I bond with Him in a mystical
union, I feel the powers of heaven
amplify as they carry me along
on the concentric waves
of the Spirit.

When all
of the trappings
and pretenses have
been shorn away; when
the façade that I have tried so
hard to construct has been swept
aside; when the outward observances
and phylacteries have been stripped from
the ritual of my worship; when the raw sores
and ugly stains of worldly influences have been
healed by the soothing balm of Gilead; when only
my true feelings remain; when I have given myself
completely and without reservation to the Lord
Jesus Christ, and only when I have yielded my
spirit to His, will I know that His grace is
sufficient, will I be able to act without
guile, and will I feel the sweet
miracle of forgiveness.

April 25

As I think about my Savior,

it causes me
pain to realize that
the parking lot at
Church is not
nearly as full
as the one
at the
mall.

It is not the exception, but
rather is the rule, that recurring
patterns of subtle self-indulgence
and the blatant neglect of our spiritual
responsibilities precipitate a loss of divine
protection. Long ago, Alexis de Tocqueville
observed: "I sought for the greatness and the
genius of America, but not until I went to her
churches and heard her pulpits aflame with
righteousness did I understand the secret
of her power. America is great because
she is good, and if she ever ceases to
be good, she will cease to be great."
When the blind lead the blind,
both will fall into the pit.

April 26

As I think about my Savior,

I determine to
become less concerned
with telestial trinkets,
and more oriented
toward celestial
sureties.

Yielding to
my base desires by
becoming locked in a fierce
competition for scarce resources,
I will surely fail to discover what it is
that will bring me happiness. The lessons
of history reveal only that both poverty and
wealth have failed miserably. Neither anonymity
nor fame seems to hold the key. Neither sickness
nor health has the ability. Both principalities and
the absence of worldly influence are inadequate.
Neither beauty nor the beast has an advantage.
I think it all comes down to this: "The dark
threads are as needful in the weaver's
skillful hand as the threads of gold
and silver in the pattern he has
planned." (B. M. Franklin).

April 27

As I think about my Savior,

the Law
of Witnesses
reaches out to me
in a personal way
that is tailored
to meet my
needs.

Witnesses
to the work and the
glory have provided me with
golden opportunities to recognize
and then to act upon my knowledge
of truth, by revealing pearls of great price
that are not readily discernible after only a
cursory glance. The shepherds in the fields,
the wise men from the East, and the Star
above Bethlehem confirm the reality of
the greatest story that has ever been
told. They were among countless
others who, since from before
the foundation of the world,
have borne testimony
of our Lord.

April 28

As I think about my Savior,

the
exercise
itself helps me
to be certain that I
take very great care
to "hearken," or give
my respectful and
even reverential
attention, to the
voice of His
counsel.

"The (very)
things which some
men esteem to be of great
worth, both to the body and
soul, others set at naught and
trample under their feet. Yea, even
the very God of Israel do men trample
under their feet. I say trample under their
feet but I would speak in other words –
they set him at naught, and hearken
not to the voice of his counsels."
(1 Nephi 19:7).

April 29

As I think about my Savior,

if I listen carefully, I can
hear the gentle rustling
of angels' wings in
the background
music of my
mind.

As the hint of
a celestial breeze ever
so slightly rustles the veil,
through its gently parted fabric
I catch a brief glimpse of those who
have come down through cloven skies
with their peaceful wings unfurled, and
I hear their heavenly music floating over
a world that has grown weary. In those
unhurried moments when my mind has
been liberated from the cares and the
concerns of the moment, the reality
of heaven is bathed in a light that
is the key to my comprehension
of the undreamed vistas of
otherwise inaccessible
experience.

April 30

As I think about my Savior,

I can
see across
time and space,
to witness the very
long shadow cast by
His star in the
East.

In the
Last Days, "the
truth of God will go forth
boldly, nobly, and independent,
till it has penetrated every continent,
visited every clime, swept every country,
and sounded in every ear; till the purposes of
God shall be accomplished, and the Great Jehovah
shall say the work is done." (Joseph Smith). In that day,
"every man shall be his own priest, and the Lord God shall
incline His ear to such. Young men shall prophesy, and
old men shall dream dreams. There will be no need
for confession in the ear, for neither the Apostles
nor they that followed many hundred years
after knew of any such whispering."
(William Tyndale).

"Blessed are they which do hunger and thirst after righteousness, for they shall be filled." (Matthew 5:6).

May 1

As I think about my Savior,

and,
from the
pulpit at Church,
I hear the laundry
list of our petitions to
Him, I realize that, for
some, the Gospel of
Jesus Christ may
simply feel like
a hearty meal,
a warm coat,
or shelter
from the
wind.

"When
I wonder
how far away
heaven is, I realize
that it's not very far.
With people like you,
it's right where you are."
(Anonymous).

May 2

As I think about my Savior

to grasp
the power of the
Atonement, I am struck
by the realization that
what I primarily need
to do is strengthen
my determination
to repetitively
repent.

If it were not possible to regularly repent of our sins, our misdeeds of the past would forever compromise our future and hold it hostage, extort our best efforts, and thwart the Great Plan of Salvation. Nephi exclaimed: "Rejoice, O my heart, and give place no more for the enemy of my soul. Do not anger again because of mine enemies. Do not slacken my strength because of mine afflictions."
(2 Nephi 4:28-30).

May 3

As I think about my Savior,

I attune my ear to the voices
of angels who quietly assure
me through the veil that
heaven's gracious Host
will usher me in to
His kingdom
of glory.

If we
are in tune
with the Spirit, we
can hear "the heavens
(as they) declare the glory
of God, and the firmament (as it)
sheweth his handiwork. (Psalms 19:1).
"His voice is heard in the rolling thunder,
and His speech is recorded in the lilac's bloom."
(Bruce R. McConkie). The earth, the sun, the moon,
and the stars "roll upon their wings in their glory, in
the midst of the power of God. All these things are
kingdoms, and any man who hath seen any or
the least of these hath seen God moving
in his majesty and power."
(D&C 84:45-47).

May 4

As I think about my Savior,

I gently brush
against the veil and
feel the presence of the
shepherds who watched
over their flocks so
long ago in the
hill country
of Judah.

I can
feel the music
of heavenly choirs as
I move in harmony with
the rhythmic waves of the Gospel
message. I hear the voices of angelic
messengers testifying that His children are
made in His image and likeness and have His
innate characteristics. I sense the Spirit with
an affinity that comes naturally, and as I
am instinctively drawn to the light, I
feel His gentle caress on my cheek,
as He brings me into His bosom
and envelops me in His
warm embrace.

May 5

As I think about my Savior,

I perform a spiritual self-diagnostic.

During the process of my self-appraisal, as my priorities are re-examined, my perceptions expand to reveal a larger view of life, my spirit is released to unlock my potential, and I yield my will to His. I find that I can tap into His power. One of my temptations is to confuse dreams with reality, but a defeat of cosmic proportion comes when my dreams are surrendered to the influences of the narrow and confining reality of the carnal and sensual world. My struggle to model my life after that of the Lord puts my behavior in harmony with Gospel principles, so that I may pursue a course that leads to improvement. In the process, I hope to find that by following the Savior's example, I will be empowered to become what I had heretofore scarcely dreamed possible. The Gospel is the perfect law of liberty, and I know that its truth can set me free to reach out and touch the stars that illuminate a celestial stage.

May 6

As I think about my Savior,

I will make the effort
to purposefully prepare
myself to greet the Sabbath
day as if it belonged to
the Lord, for so
it does.

For
some, it
is no more than
a day off work. But it
should be a day of recreation,
when we can literally re-create or
re-invent ourselves in His image. Those
who profane or secularize the Sabbath are no
longer put to death, and yet their progression is
halted because they die spiritually when their
imprudent behavior has alienated them from
His influence. The seventh day of the week
was envisioned as a work-release program
to see how we would behave if we were
left on our own, after having received
instruction regarding what we
ought to be doing.

May 7

As I think about my Savior,

I am given
an opportunity
to reflect upon just
how bountifully He
has blessed me, both
temporally and
spiritually.

The distance that we must
travel in order for us to return
to our heavenly home is measured
in faith, and not in miles or in currency.
That path will be punctuated by service and
memorialized by sacrifice. If our religion does
not require the surrender of our will to a higher
authority, it can never generate the power to save
our souls. Agency may be the hallmark of the
Plan, but sooner or later, we are all going to
have Gethsemane experiences. How we
react to those epiphanies will provide
our Father in Heaven with an
accurate measurement of
our core testimony
temperature.

May 8

As I think about my Savior,

I recall how, during His ministry
among the Nephites, multitudes
were baptized with fire and
with the Holy Ghost.

For
those present,
it must have been a
pentecostal experience,
for "they were encircled
about as if it were by fire; and
it came down from heaven, and
the multitude did witness it, and did
bear record; and angels did come down
out of heaven and did minister unto them."
(3 Nephi 19:14). It was as it had been during
the Exodus, when Moses was commanded:
"Put off thy shoes from off thy feet, for the
place whereon thou standest is holy
ground. For I am the God of thy
fathers, the God of Abraham,
the God of Isaac, and the
God of Jacob."
(Exodus 3:5-6).

May 9

As I think about my Savior,

I feel more profoundly "what
love the Father hath showed
upon us, that we should
be called His sons."
(William Tyndale).

Elohim is
my Father, and I was
born of Him as His spirit
child. I inherited His qualities of
nobility and graciousness, and was
raised by Him to maturity, until I could
progress no further. I then departed from
His presence to experience life on this earth
that He had created, because there were some
laws that pertain only to mortality that I could
not have beforehand obeyed, and so there were
some blessings that were as yet unavailable to
me. As a result of my faithful determination
to fulfill a mortal mission, I now have the
assurance of a physical resurrection, as
well as the opportunity to enjoy
eternal life with my extended
family in the Celestial
Kingdom.

May 10

As I think about my Savior,

I
engage
His power
to wean me
from milk to
meat.

My
expanding
spiritual awareness
demands an answer to
the question: "Where did I
come from?" "I am God," the
Lord told Moses. "I made the
world, and all men before they
were in the flesh." (Moses 6:51).
He revealed to Jeremiah: "Before
I formed thee in the belly I knew
thee; and before thou camest forth
out of the womb I sanctified thee,
and I ordained thee (that thou
might one day be) a prophet
unto the nations."
(Jeremiah 1:4-5).

May 11

As I think about my Savior,

I acknowledge the often unappreciated power of the weak things of the earth.

It is very likely that my survival will depend upon what I do with my weakness, as well as on what that weakness does to me. I may allow it to either impede or facilitate my progress. I am fortunate, indeed, if the Savior intervenes and laces my weakness with healthy measures of humility in order to transform my narrow perspective, so that I might see supposed stumbling blocks as the very stepping stones that are needed to reinforce my confidence and conquer my timidity.

May 12

As I think about my Savior,

I receive an external heart
massage that is soothing to
my spirit, leaving me
to enjoy a divine
perspective.

As long as
I retain a memory
of my former life and the
purpose of my call, when my
best laid plans go awry, I can hold
fast to the promise that "the Lord shall
come, and his recompense shall be with him,
and he shall reward me" with a measure that is
equal to my labors. (D&C 56:19). Although it may
remain my natural inclination to feather my own
nest during my sojourn through mortality, I will
try to remember the caution about becoming too
concerned with my lot in life. For, even though
the Savior "will refresh us during our journey
through life with some pleasant inns, He
will not encourage us to mistake
them for" our real "home."
(C.S. Lewis).

May 13

As I think about my Savior,

I recognize the truth in His declaration,
that "inasmuch as ye have done it unto
one of the least of these, my brethren,
ye have done it unto me."
(Matthew 25:40).

I
patiently
bear my stripes for
the Savior. I try to go the
second mile, and struggle to serve
Him. I make every attempt to love my
neighbors as myself. I visit those in prison.
I minister to the weak, the sick and infirm, and
I clothe those who are naked, because of my desire to
stand in His stead. I bear His name when I go about His
errand because He has awakened within me an appreciation
of my commitments, and has helped me to be more alive to
my responsibilities. Even when I pause in my efforts, I can
sense His presence, because I still feel my pulse racing
with the conscious awareness that it is He Who has
quickened me and given vitality to my life. I hope
that I will always be able to feel in the beat of
my heart His conjoint ownership in the
accomplishment of my commission.

May 14

As I think about my Savior,

I feel my blood stir, as I sense that the days
are unfolding, when He will come again
in the clouds, to meet the Church
of the Firstborn.

His disciples
patiently acknowledge
His timetable, while the world
insists on instant carnal satisfaction
and immediate gratification through the
natural senses. In the presence of burning bushes,
disciples remove the latchets from their shoes, while
Babylon is preoccupied with the occult, diviners, magic,
and soothsayers. She rolls the dice, dreaming of the riches
that will be hers if only her lucky number comes up. His
disciples stand in holy places and are not moved, while
Babylon rattles her sabers and appropriates money for
military preparedness in a false sense of security that
is curiously supported by a MAD policy of Mutually
Assured Destruction, that is, in turn, backed up
by a stockpile of weapons with the potential
to unleash the power of creation itself.
Babylon has "become Death, the
destroyer of worlds."
(Vishnu).

May 15

As I think about my Savior,

I catch a glimpse of what
it means to enjoy the
companionship
of the Spirit.

What I am
seeking is nothing
less than His Rest, or a
sanctuary that is born of a
settled conviction in my mind
of the truth. Today, I may enter
into God's Rest by harnessing for
good my grasp of Gospel principles,
and by then being true to His celestial
laws. The peace that then surpasses all
understanding flows from a unity that
eludes the world because it is alien to
carnal minds. When the Spirit brings
me to a correct comprehension of the
nature of God, I will find that I am
poised to embark on a journey of
eternal progression leading all
the way to the portals of His
Celestial Kingdom.

May 16

As I think about my Savior,

I want to sit
at the feet of the
prophets and feel their
vibrant testimonies
animate my
spirit.

It is
one thing to
keep in mind the
relationship of God
with His children from
the beginning. Those events
that were prophesied long ago
and have since come to pass serve
to confirm our faith and strengthen our
testimony that He maintains a relationship
with His children. It is quite another thing to
sit at the feet of latter-day prophets, seers, and
revelators, who teach the body of known truth,
interpret and clarify hidden truth, and reveal
new or forgotten truth, all by the power
and authority of the priesthood
that bears His holy name.

May 17

As I think about my Savior,

the innocence of His
character acutely contrasts
with the guilt and pain
that accompany my
disobedience.

My
unresolved sin
is an unquenchable
fire that leaves my hope
for happiness in ashes. David O.
McKay taught: "The first condition
of happiness is a clear conscience." In
physical terms, before my wounds can heal,
they have to be clean. The development of my
character will obey the same principles. As I
strive to achieve optimal spiritual health, I
must first attend to festering sores that
would otherwise erode my resistance
to the infection of my soul. There
can be no skeletons lurking in
the closet, waiting to scare
the living daylights
out of me.

May 18

As I think about my Savior,

I recall
with sobriety
that "the wages of
sin is death, but the
gift of God is eternal
life, through Jesus
Christ our Lord."
(Romans 6:23).

"I had rather
be a doorkeeper in
the house of my God, than
to dwell in the tents of wickedness."
(Psalms 84:10). It is good to sometimes
work without pay behind the scenes and far
from media attention, without recognition,
recompense, or reciprocation. It can be
liberating to enjoy the refreshment
of a celestial breeze that cools
our faces when they have
been moistened with
the perspiration
of honest
toil.

May 19

As I think about my Savior,

I can more clearly make out the
grey-toned obstacles to my progression,
that stand out in sharp contrast to the
Technicolor backdrop of the Plan
that God has created for me.

It
is quite
clear to me that
the most daunting
enemy that I will ever
encounter is within myself.
I must confront and overcome
that obstacle first, and bring my
conduct into strict obedience to the
principles of Heavenly Father's Plan.
For it is a clearly defined road map that
allows me to follow a trail of deliberately
scattered star dust in the direction of my
dreams. If we want to reach Neverland,
all we need to do is take the "second
star to the right, and (continue)
straight on 'til morning!"
("Peter Pan").

May 20

As I think about my Savior,

I remember the
powerful testimony of His
faithful witness Isaiah,
and hear the messages
of old speaking to
me from out of
the dust.

There is an
interesting account
of the discovery of the Bar
Kokhba Documents, that were
hidden in caves near Ein Gedi on the
western shore of the Salt Sea, about 131 A.D.
These records were deliberately buried deeply in
the dry earth of the cave floor, and when they came
to light there were choking clouds of dust, so that
the archaeologists had to wear masks in order
to breathe. Truly, the voices of the prophets
call to us "out of the ground," their
speech is "low out of the dust,"
and we hear them whisper
to us "out of the dust."
(Isaiah 29:4).

May 21

As I think about my Savior,

I realize that
I have a date with
destiny, and know that
in a not too distant day,
I will stand revealed,
before my Maker.

I
cannot lie
to God, for since
the very moment of
my birth, angels have
been taking silent notes
as the conduct of my life
unfolds before their eyes.
Besides, I write the record
of my days in the sinews of
my body and in the tablet
of my mind. In a coming
day, it will be unfolded
before Him, for He can
interpret that history
as easily as I can
read a book.

May 22

As I think about my Savior,

I review my own efforts
to achieve mastery in
the curriculum of
the Gospel.

When I was
born, I began my
earthly schooling in
the Kindergarten of God,
and I was as a child in Primary.
I was trailing clouds of glory, for I
had just come from my heavenly home.
Years have now passed, and the graduation
ceremony that will mark the conclusion of my
course of study draws ever closer. It is comforting to
know that, when I cross the bar to enter the kingdom
of God, my body will "be full of light. (3 Nephi 13:22).
But I might be quite surprised to discover that I will
enjoy no more intrinsic luminosity then, than any
three year old in Sunbeam class has now. As the
Savior so insightfully taught, "Suffer the
little children, and forbid them not,
to come unto me: for of such is
the kingdom of heaven."
(Mark 10:14).

May 23

As I think about my Savior,

I will lift up my voice in
both song and in story,
even as He causes
banners of peace
to be unfurled
throughout
the world.

"I'd like to build
the world a home and
furnish it with love. Grow apple
trees and honey bees, and snow-white
turtle doves. I'd like to teach the world to sing
in perfect harmony. I'd like to hold it in my arms,
and keep it company." ("The New Seekers"). Diplomats
may seek peaceful solutions to conflict, even as antagonists
jockey for position to gain an advantage, but there will be
no harmony in the world until the supremacy of the
Prince of Peace is universally recognized, and
until every contending faction extends the
olive branch and acknowledges its
individual responsibility and
accepts accountability
for its behavior.

May 24

As I think about my Savior,

I am given the opportunity
to review and renew my
testimony of His
divinity and
mission.

For my
part, I believe
in Christ. I speak and
testify of His foreordination
to be the Redeemer of the world.
In His baptism, He demonstrated by
example the way for all to follow. In His
ministry, He taught in simplicity the truths
of the Gospel. In the Garden of Gethsemane, He
demonstrated His strength and compassion. The
crucifixion, then, was only an apostrophe; His
death but a pause to re-focus attention on His
resurrection and ascension into heaven. He
is my Advocate with the Father, the Bread
of Life, the Cornerstone of my creation,
the Rock of my redemption, and
the Foundation of my
existence.

May 25

As I think about my Savior,

I am moved to follow His example in meekness, and in lowliness of heart, and in humility.

Try as I might, I will never be able to express to Him enough gratitude for all that I am and ever will be. Although I may serve Him with all my soul, yet I will remain an unprofitable servant. That is because my debt to Him is completely beyond my ability to pay. But rather than requiring me to settle my account with Him, He asks only that I keep His commandments. The miracle is that the greater is my obedience, the more He blesses me. Thus, I become even more deeply indebted to Him and I will remain so forever. Ultimately, when I have been redeemed by His precious blood, it will be by His grace, and that alone, that I will enjoy salvation.

May 26

As I think about my Savior,

I acknowledge that I have been
emboldened and empowered
by an evolving drama, set on
a world stage, that may
seem incredible
to others.

All of us have
"limiting beliefs," those
stories we tell ourselves that
cause us to sabotage our own best
efforts. They haunt us as they diminish
our abilities and obscure our goals. Many
people don't realize it's possible to change them,
and, for that matter, may not even realize that they
have them. Breaking free from limiting beliefs can
unleash the power of our potential, and release
the pixie dust that has the magic to vitalize
our wits, to energize them so that they
may grow sharper, that we may
recognize, appreciate, and
even harness the elusive
power and authority
of God.

May 27

As I think about my Savior,

I pause in my perennial
efforts to exhaust myself in
trivial pursuits, and realize that
if I will just step back, take a deep
breath, and resolve to endure
in righteousness, I will
ultimately enjoy
His Rest.

The
only way for
me to prepare for
that day is to conform
my life to the Plan of God.
When I have gained a perfect
testimony of the divinity of the
work, and when I no longer suffer
from fear, doubt, the religious turmoil
of the world, or from the vagaries of men,
I will enter into God's Rest. That peace
will be born of my settled conviction
of the truth, and will follow my
obedience to celestial
principles.

May 28

As I think about my Savior,

I marvel how the
principle of happiness
has been so thoughtfully
stitched into the fabric of His
coat of many colors, and that it
has been individual tailored
to fit me perfectly.

"The
dark threads
are as needful in the
weaver's skillful hand as
the threads of gold and silver,
in the pattern he has planned."
(Benjamin M. Franklin). But when
I accept the invitation to try the virtue
of His word, I will be exposed to both the
innovative stitchery and luxuriant texture of
the cloth that He has cut for me, and I will
throw open my senses to the realm of
joy that may be experienced only
by those who have elected to
be obedient to Gospel
principles.

May 29

As I think about my Savior,

I am moved to
embrace the covenants
that He has provided, that
I might fully partake of
His divine nature.

I may have
already come a long
way, but as I reach out to
touch the face of God, my real
journey to Christ will have only just
begun. I must continue to press forward
with complete dedication and steadfastness,
with confidence and a firm brightness of hope.
I must extend my love, not only to Him, but also
to all my brothers and sisters. As I feast upon the
scriptures and from them receive strength and
nourishment, as holy contracts secure for me
the blessings of heaven, and as I endure to
the end in righteousness, I shall finally
receive a full measure of His grace
and enjoy life with Him in His
kingdom, which, of all His
gifts, is the greatest.

May 30

As I think about my Savior,

a widening
smile becomes my
passport to adventure, as
I learn to appreciate the
wonders that He has
created for my
enjoyment.

The clear and
unmistakable word of the
Lord came to Brigham Young at
Winter Quarters: "If thou art merry,
praise the Lord with singing, with music,
with dancing, and with a prayer of praise and
thanksgiving." (D&C 136:28). It is amazing how
our laughter and our smiles can speak a universal
language. When we are happy, we are moved by
the tempo of harmonious melodies of Gospel
rhythms and motivated to shift into higher
spiritual gears. Our launch pads are
left behind, as we are propelled
upward on the concentric
waves of the
spirit.

May 31

As I think about my Savior,

even my
most faltering
and hesitant prayers
have the power to
bind me to the
Infinite.

"The builder
who first bridged
Niagara's gorge, before
he swung his cable shore to
shore, sent out across the gulf his
venturing kite, bearing a slender cord
for unseen hands to grasp upon the further
cliff and draw a greater cord, and then a greater
yet, 'til at last across the chasm swung the cable -
then the mighty bridge in air. So may we send our
little timid thoughts across the void, out to God's
reaching hands. Send out our love and faith to
thread the deep, thought after thought, until
the little cord has greatened to a chain no
chance can break, and we are anchored
to the Infinite." (Edward Markham).

"Blessed are the pure in heart,
for they shall see God."
(Matthew 5:8).

June 1

As I think about my Savior,

I learn
how to use
the power of His
word, so that I may
wield it like a two
edged sword,
to separate
truth from
error.

And
yet, as a
true disciple, I
still pray for those
who refuse to believe,
and who find fault with
the Church, whose unchecked
behavior will ultimately be their
own undoing. How sad it will be
when they finally admit: "It
ain't my ignorance that
done me in, but what
I knowed that
warn't so."

June 2

As I think about my Savior,

it is not
necessary to look any
further than to places of
quiet refuge, of shelter from
the winds of adversity and
the wiles of the adversary,
where I can go to find the
composure as well as the
inspiration to create
heaven on earth
and be not
moved.

A holy
place has more to
do with how we live
than where we live. If we
are striving to do our duty,
then surely we are standing in
a holy place, which is anywhere
that we enjoy the presence
and companionship
of the Spirit of
God.

June 3

As I think about my Savior,

as an heir of
the Abrahamic
Covenant, and as
His faithful subject,
I affirm that He was
born King of
the Jews.

We can be
sure that, in the not too
distant future, all of the children
of Israel will recognize Him as their
Messiah. And so, "by the authority of His
priesthood that has again been restored to the
earth, and by the ministration under the direction
of the Prophet of God, Apostles of the Lord Jesus Christ
have been to the Holy Land and have dedicated that
country for the return of the Jews; and we believe
that in the due time of the Lord they shall be in
the favor of God again. And let no Latter-day
Saint be guilty of taking any part in any
crusade against these people." (Heber
J. Grant, in 1921, 27 years before
the creation of the State
of Israel).

June 4

As I think about my Savior,

I will pay
more than just
lip service to the
invitation of angels
in heaven to give
"glory to God in
the highest!"
(Luke 2:14).

Theirs is a
solicitation to
come unto Jesus,
and to develop my
own sure witness of the
truth. To that end, I need
look no further than to the
simple instructions given by
His servants in the scriptures.
One recommended that I "ask
with a sincere heart, with real
intent, having faith in Christ."
(Moroni 10:4). The counsel of
another was that I "ask in
faith, nothing wavering."
(James 1:6).

June 5

As I think about my Savior,

I am repeatedly taught by the Spirit this simple truth: "Neither is there any respect of persons with him."
(William Tyndale).

I hope to learn that "He is indifferent and not partial; as great in His sight is a servant as a master." (William Tyndale). There are no ordinary people, and "you have never talked to a mere mortal. It is immortals with whom we joke, work, marry, snub and exploit. Our charity must be a real and costly love; no mere tolerance or indulgence which parodies love as flippancy parodies merriment. Next to the blessed sacrament itself, your neighbor is the holiest object presented to your senses, for in him also Christ is truly hidden and glorified." (C.S. Lewis).
As Jean Valjean said after a lifetime of searching: "To love another person is to see the face of God." (Victor Hugo, "Les Miserables").

June 6

As I think about my Savior,

in my mind, I can hear all the bells
of Christendom ringing out in an
appeal for peace on earth and
good will toward men.

There
will be peace on
earth only after the Saints
have been tried and tested in the
fiery crucible of mortal experience.
They will look to the Lord Jesus Christ as a
living testament to the potential for goodness
that can be found in all of us. Their example will
illustrate that the reward of faith is celestial surety,
while the price of fear is telestial uncertainty. They
will give value, instead of taking what they can get.
They will stand for accountability, in contrast to a
flight from responsibility, and will embrace a
work ethic, instead of unappreciated and
undeserved entitlement. Their spiritual
maturity will prevail over juvenile
irresponsibility, and there will
be peace on earth and good
will toward men.

June 7

As I think about my Savior,

although
I may find myself
in the midst of tumultuous
telestial traffic, a cacophony of
confusion, and a world that is
in commotion from ocean to
ocean, I am able to stand
above the fray and
hear the voices
of angels.

I try to be meek
and submissive as I join with
His ever-faithful disciple William
Tyndale, and continue my labors to
gain "knowledge, understanding, and
feeling, (while I) beware superstition
and persuasion of worldly wisdom,
philosophy, and of hypocrisy and
ceremonies." As the Lord begins
to enlighten my unfettered
mind, I will walk in the
plain and open
truth.

June 8

As I think about my Savior,

I commit
myself to Him with
all my heart, might,
mind, and strength;
to take up my cross
and follow Him,
wherever that
path might
lead.

In over 200
scriptural verses, the
prophets have employed the
beautiful expression "Saints" to
describe those who believe in the
Savior and have endured the crosses
of the world. Joseph Smith's translation
of Matthew 16:24 provides us with a clear
definition of what it means to "take up our
cross." According to his interpretation, the
Lord explained: "It is to deny (ourselves)
all ungodliness, and every worldly lust,
and keep (His) commandments."
(J.S.T. Matthew 16:26).

June 9

As I think about my Savior,

I
can see
that He is the
greatest gift my
Father could
have given
me.

My
gratitude
to Heavenly
Father is much
deeper than thanks.
Thankfulness is just the
beginning of gratitude and
may consist only of words, but
gratitude is shown in action. It is
independent of circumstances and
penetrates deeply to the underlying
currents of life. It interacts personally
and even intimately with my Maker,
and is contingent upon neither
recognition, recompense,
or reciprocation.

June 10

As I think about my Savior,

to all with ears to hear, I
testify of the indisputable
supremacy of His might,
majesty, power, and
dominion over
all the earth.

I am
in awe that
He would be willing
to delegate responsibility
to one such as I. But how could I
be expected to learn about the righteous
exercise of power, "except in this laboratory
of life setting? Could we have truly experienced
both the risks and opportunities of power merely
by attending some pointed lectures or by doing some
directed reading during our first estate? Was it not
necessary to experience what it is like to be on
the receiving end of unrighteous dominion,
as well as to understand the necessity
of repentance when one has been
been on the giving end?"
(Neal A. Maxwell).

June 11

As I think about my Savior,

I am
sensitive to the
subtle reminders
given by the Spirit
that He is present in
all that I believe, and
that He should be my
invited guest, to be
with me in all my
thoughts, and in
all that I say
and do.

If there can be
found no guile within
our hearts, it will be our privilege
to "have confidence toward God. And
whatsoever we ask, we (shall) receive of
Him, because we keep His commandments,
and do those things that are pleasing" to
Him. We have faith, and believe "on
the name of his Son Jesus Christ,
and love one another."
(1 James 3:21-23).

June 12

As I think about my Savior,

I recognize that
He was once a child, as
we are also "the children of
God." Because of our lineage,
we are "heirs of God, and
joint heirs with Christ."
(Romans 8:16-17).

I am
confident that I
will "receive a crown
of glory that fadeth not
away." (1 Peter 5:4). For I am
the offspring "of the living God."
(Hosea 1:10). "The Spirit itself beareth
witness with our spirit, that we are the
children of God." (Romans 8:16). I feel
within me a yearning to know: "Have
we not all one father? Hath not one
God created us?" (Malachi 2:10).
The answer resonates within
my heart: Of a truth, He
is the "Father of all."
(Ephesians 4:6).

June 13

As I think about my Savior,

I am
given the
chance to clear
my mind and
reassess my
priorities.

I
lose power
and purpose when
my priorities are out of
order. This is why it has been
necessary for the Lord to clarify
His Gospel in successive periods of
time called "Dispensations." He wants
our perspective to be unambiguous, so that
we can focus on the principles of perfection that
are validated by the Spirit as they are revealed by
the tongues of angels who have come from His
heavenly throne, and are then taught by His
servants whose power and authority He
always carefully restores following
recurring episodes of spiritual
neglect, or apostasy.

June 14

As I think about my Savior,

rather than
shuttering my windows
and bolting the door, I will
throw them open to my friends
and neighbors, and invite
them into the warmth
of my faith and
fellowship.

"So
much depends
upon our willingness
to" wake up and smell the
roses, "to make up our minds
collectively and individually that
present levels of performance are
not acceptable, either to ourselves
or to the Lord. In saying that, I am
not calling for flashy, temporary
differences.....but for a quiet
resolve to do a better job
to lengthen our stride."
(Spencer W. Kimball).

June 15

As I think about my Savior

with
an eternal
perspective, I
will resist the
temptation to
put my trust
in gods of
wood or
stone.

Materialism
is a plaque that
will clog my spiritual
arteries. Focusing on the
work of the Kingdom is an
angioplasty that can help me
to regain my perspective and
strengthen my admiration for
the nobility of God's mission
statement: To bring to pass
my immortality and my
eternal life in His
kingdom.

June 16

As I think about my Savior,

I
yield to Him
that which has
been hardest for
me to give up:
My former
self.

I may be an
independent agent
with freedom to choose,
but the decision to escape the
the consequences of my poor choices
is not an option. The immutable Law of
the Harvest expects my performance to be
carried out within the context of the Gospel.
Otherwise, poor choices and bad habits will
lead to my enslavement. The redeeming
act of God waits upon my initiative to
put off my fallen nature and to come
unto Him. Every step of the way,
and at every turn in the road,
He preserves agency as the
hallmark of His Plan.

June 17

As I think about my Savior,

and listen
to His apostles
bear testimony
of His divinity, I
receive a quiet
confirmation
from the
Spirit.

The nature of
the Apostolic calling
is to bear witness to all
the world of the divinity
of the Savior, and to teach
the way to salvation and to
exaltation, in ways that are
powerfully communicated
by the Holy Ghost so that,
without the need for any
additional endorsement,
their messages may be
easily understood by
the heart, as well as
by the head.

June 18

As I think about my Savior

and the
shepherds who
tended their flocks
in the pastures near
Bethlehem, I remember
how an angel of the Lord
came upon them, so much
so, that "the glory of the
Lord shone round
about them."
(Luke 2:9).

As I
quietly listen to
the whisperings of the
Spirit, I feel that angels will
attend me, as well, and that
"whoever speaks to me in the
right voice, him or her I shall
follow as the waters follow
the moon, silently, with
fluid steps, anywhere
around the globe."
(Walt Whitman).

June 19

As I think about my Savior,

I remember
those who have
gone before me, to
whom I owe a great
debt of gratitude
for selfless acts
of sacrifice.

William Tyndale stated to a cleric
of his day: "If God spare my life, ere
long I shall cause a plough boy to know the
scriptures better than you do!" This humble priest,
who lived five centuries ago, was able to look through
the mists of time to see the present day. He knew me. He
used the symbol of an illiterate plough boy to illustrate not
only his divinely inspired commission to translate the Bible
into the language of the people, but also to jar me out of my
complacency and indifference, that I might use the gift he
has given me at great cost, to read the scriptures in my
own tongue. In a few years, we will commemorate
the 500th anniversary of the printing of his Bible.
I hope to be ready for the celebration, and that
my scholarship will be evidence that he
did not labor, or die, in vain.

June 20

As I think about my Savior,

I pause to
consider that
He was born
to give me
a second
birth.

The
spirit of
forgiveness
is "promised
unto all, so that
whosoever repenteth
is immediately beloved
of God." (William Tyndale).
That same spirit came upon the
people of Zarahemla, who "were
filled with joy, having received
a remission of their sins, and
having peace of conscience,
because of the exceeding
faith which they had
in Jesus Christ."
(Mosiah 4:3).

June 21

As I think about my Savior,

I can
almost feel His
gentle touch as He
reaches out to me to
calm my troubled
soul, like a bridge
over troubled
waters.

When I feel
His presence, I
am bathed in vitality
and am empowered with
an otherworldly serenity. As
Bagheera, the powerfully built
black panther confided to Mowgli
the man-cub: "I had never seen the
jungle. They fed me behind bars from
an iron pan until one night I felt that
I was Bagheera the Panther, and no
man's plaything, and I broke the
lock with one blow of my
paw, and I came away."
("The Jungle Book").

June 22

As I think about my Savior,

I want to
be a deserving
recipient of His
divine spirit of
forgiveness.

It has been deviously
said that revenge is a dish
that is best served cold, when
we are no longer caught up in the
heat of the moment, but can afford
to be crafty, cunning, and calculating
as we plot our payback. But it is still like
swallowing poison and hoping it will kill
the other guy. The word "revenge" is found
just thirteen times in the scriptures, but the
word "forgive" is found one hundred fifty
five times. When Peter asked: "Lord, how
oft shall my brother sin against me, and
I forgive him? till seven times? Jesus
saith unto him, I say not unto thee,
until seven times: but, until
seventy times seven."
(Matthew 18:20-21).

June 23

As I think about my Savior,

I
determine to
make conscious efforts
to help my brethren "to bear
their weakness, to be courteous
unto them, and to win them
unto Christ, and overcome
them with kindness."
(William Tyndale).

We should always
be ready to offer hope and
encouragement, and to speak kind
words, to awaken cheerfulness in the
souls of others, "til heart meets with heart
and rejoices in friendship that ever is true."
(Joseph Townsend). Charity must be founded
on forgiveness, triggered by tolerance, reflected
in respect, and affected by appreciation. Our
gentle expressions can be the keywords
that will trigger a response from the
angels in heaven, who are waiting
to part the veil and lead us
to the riches of eternity.

June 24

As I think about my Savior,

the
Spirit renews
the promise that in
a coming day, we shall
leave behind us this vale
of tears, to inherit a new
heaven and a new
earth.

As
difficult
as our lot in
life may seem,
it is not likely that
many of us would trade
places with those trailblazers
who have preceded us. Instead
of a terrifying spectre of martyr's
fires, truth now burns brightly. We
all pray that never again will the great
and abominable church of the devil wield
the power and influence to "suffer no man
to know God's word, but burn it and make
heresy of it." (William Tyndale).

June 25

As I think about my Savior,

the stunning
clarity of His doctrine
strikes a familiar chord
as it bathes me in
its dazzling
light.

Those
who have had the
privilege to be taught by
the Spirit often stare in wide-
eyed wonder at the mesmerizing
simplicity of interwoven threads that
are found within the intricate pattern of
Gospel principles. These comprise a coat of
many colors that, taken as a whole, is nothing
less than the Technicolor tapestry of the Great
Plan of Salvation. Full spectrum revelatory
experiences will always stand out boldly
against the monochromatic and slit-
eyed skepticism with which the
unrepentant and hard
hearted confront
the truth.

June 26

As I think about my Savior,

I can feel the
delicate tracings of the
divine pattern that has been
woven into the fabric
of my sinews.

Mortality has
been pointedly designed
to be a life-long work project
that gives me the opportunity to mold
my nature to more closely resemble that of
God. My freedom to choose in an atmosphere so
full of dangerous deceptions, enticing entrapments,
perilous pathways, and soothing seductions entails great
risk. There are, however, places of refuge that are untainted
from the blood and sins of this generation, where I may flee
from Spiritual Babylon; places where I may shelter my soul,
grasp the horns of sanctuary, quiet my racing heart, and
ease the tensions that build up when I have allowed
myself to get caught up in the fast lane of life;
places where I may pause to quietly reflect
upon the quality of my preparation to
live in harmony with my Heavenly
Father for all eternity.

June 27

As I think about my Savior,

I receive His assurance
that the Spirit will safely
guide me back to my
heavenly home.

"Lo, saith He,
I am with you always,
even unto the end of the world."
(William Tyndale). I am not alone, now or
ever. In fact, "Adam fell that men might be, and
men are that they might have joy." (2 Nephi 2:25).
Our natural expectation is to relish endless felicity in
the comfortable environment of the eternal realm to
which we all aspire. But we want to find happiness
during our sojourn here on earth, as well, even as
we labor diligently to merit our golden ticket. The
good news we have all been longing to hear is
that we can have our cake and eat it too. We
were created so that we might experience
joy not only in the resurrection, but also
during the brief interlude of mortality.
This is one of the many reassuring
revelations that are the real
gifts of the Restoration.

June 28

As I think about my Savior,

I am moved to ask
Him to receive all of His
children into His tender
care, and to keep them
fit to live with Him
in His heavenly
home.

At the time of the post-mortal
ministry of Jesus Christ, in the vicinity
of the temple in the land of Bountiful, the
Saints brought their children to the Savior, that
He might minister to them. After taking them "one
by one" in His arms, He "blessed them, and prayed
unto the Father for them." (3 Nephi 17:21). The Spirit
was overwhelming. As the multitude raised their eyes
to the heavens, the veil itself parted, "and they saw
angels descending out of heaven as it were in the
midst of fire; and they came down and encircled
those little ones…with fire. And the angels
did minister unto them." (3 Nephi 17:24).
Truly, they were "one, the Children of
Christ, and heirs to the kingdom
of God." (4 Nephi 1:17).

June 29

As I think about my Savior,

I am able
to spend some
"alone time" with
Him, and to rejoice
in my individuality
as one of our Father's
unique creations.

I realize
that God has made
each one of us with a specific
purpose in mind. So, "here's to the
kids who are different, the kids who don't
always get A^s; the kids who have ears twice the
size of their peers, and noses that go on for days.
Here's to the kids who are different, the kids they
call crazy or dumb; the kids who don't fit, with
the guts and the grit; who dance to a different
drum. Here's to the kids who are different,
the kids with the mischievous streak. For
when they have grown, as history has
shown, it's their difference that
makes them unique."
(Digby Wolfe).

June 30

As I think about my Savior,

my vision
is recalibrated
to see Him in the
beauty of spring-time
flowers that wave in
the wind beneath
sun-swept
skies.

"Oh, I have slipped
the surly bonds of earth
and danced the skies on laughter
silvered wings. Sunward I've climbed,
and joined the tumbling mirth of sun split
clouds, and done a hundred things you have
not dreamed of; wheeled and soared and swung
high in the sunlit silence. Hovering there, I've chased
the shouting wind along, and flung my eager craft through
footless halls of air. Up, up the long, delirious, burning blue
I've topped the windswept heights with easy grace, where
never lark, or even eagle flew. And, while with silent,
lifting mind I've trod the high untrespassed sanctity
of space, I put out my hand, and touched the
face of God." (John G. Magee, Jr.).

"Blessed are the peacemakers,
for they shall be called the children of God."
(Matthew 5:9).

July 1

As I think about my Savior,

the
Spirit
confirms
that I have
been Born
Again.

All of those
who have renounced the
world and have entered into
the Covenant "are born of him."
(Mosiah 5:7). Covenants are binding
contracts between ourselves and God.
Therefore, no person may enter into such
except on the basis of revelation from God,
and upon the exercise of priesthood power
by His authorized servants who have been
ordained to administer the ordinances
of the Gospel. When these conditions
have been met, those in the embrace
of fidelity and fraternity with
the Savior are described as
having been "Born
Again."

July 2

As I think about my Savior,

I
marvel that
the Restoration of
His Gospel in the Last
Days has awakened all
the earth from a deep
slumber after a
long night of
darkness.

It can be our
calm assurance that
"no unhallowed hand can"
at this point "stop the work from
progressing. Persecutions may rage,
mobs may combine, armies may assemble,
calumny may defame, but the truth of God will
go forth boldly, nobly, and independent, until it
has penetrated every continent, visited every
clime, swept every country, and sounded in
every ear, 'til the purposes of God shall be
accomplished and the Great Jehovah
shall say: 'The work is done.'"
(Joseph Smith).

July 3

As I think about my Savior,

spam
goes directly
into the trash,
even as my in-box
regularly receives a
flood of notable
emails from
Home.

These are the
"love letters" I receive
from God. "Thou hast had
signs enough," Alma counseled
Korihor: "All things that are upon
the face of (the earth) do witness that
there is a Supreme Creator." (Alma 30:44).
Certainly, "any man who hath seen any or
the least of these hath seen God moving in
his majesty and power." (D&C 88:48). As
Emerson commented: "How does nature
deify us with a few and cheap elements!
Give me health and a day, and I will
make the pomp of emperors
ridiculous."

July 4

As I think about my Savior,

I am in awe of His ability and His willingness to assume my debts, negotiate the price of my deliverance, and arrange the pointedly specific terms of my redemption.

I recognize the truth of the statement that "if ye by the grace of God are perfect in Christ, and deny not his power, then are ye sanctified in Christ by the grace of God, through the shedding of the blood of Christ, which is in the covenant of the Father unto the remission of your sins, that ye become holy, without spot." (Moroni 10:33). It would be difficult to express more succinctly, and yet more powerfully, the ability of the Gospel, that is central to the Merciful Plan of our Father, to perfect my life.

July 5

As I think about my Savior,

the stage
is set for the
Holy Ghost to
give me just the
divine tutorial
training that
I need.

As the
Spirit enlarges
my understanding,
the word of God will bloom
with hidden meanings I hadn't
been aware of, as their applications
pop into my mind in relevant situations
just when I need them the most. In a
wonderfully whole and complete
way, the Lord will be responsive
to my feeble efforts to seek out
His guidance. As I learn to
draw upon His virtue, I
will reach out, as it
were, and touch
His garment.

July 6

As I think about my Savior,

I
realize that
I am living on a
spiritual credit; that
in a coming day,
my account will
be closed, and
an equitable
settlement
will be
made.

"My father
focuses heart-gripping
flashes across the wall screen.
Family slides. I am small, my brother
is smaller, my sister is smallest. Days now
dead re-open like old storybooks from memory's
heaped box. Soberly, I think of another Father, Who
someday shall open my mind, and flash reeling
remembering of every day's minute across
my soul, across the heavens, and
kindly ask me to narrate."
(Lora Lyn Stucker).

July 7

As I think about my Savior,

I am comforted
to link my testimony
with the words of His
faithful witnesses of old,
who were "inspired from
heaven" and who were
"sent forth, standing
among the people
in all the land."
(3 Nephi 6:20).

"We are
weak and simple
and unlearned," declared
one of His apostles. "Of ourselves
we can do nothing, but in the strength
of the Lord we cannot fail. It is His power
that sustains and guides us. Our position or
status or divine commission is no different than
that of the prophets and apostles of old. We
also are the agents of the Lord, are His
ambassadors, and we are, as were
they, His legal administrators."
(Bruce R. McConkie).

July 8

As I think about my Savior,

I am
drawn into
the safe haven of His
protective influence, and
am shielded from the anguish
that so often accompanies the
recognition of opportunities
that have been lost, and of
hopes and dreams that
might never be
realized.

"But you
were always a good
man of business, Jacob." said
Scrooge. "Business!" cried the ghost,
wringing its hands again. "Mankind was
my business. The common welfare was my
business. Charity, mercy, forbearance, and
benevolence were all my business. The
dealings of my trade were but a drop
of water in the comprehensive
ocean of my business."
("A Christmas Carol").

July 9

As I think about my Savior,

I view
adversity,
my trials and
tribulations, as
tailor-made
gifts from
God.

The day is at hand
that I find myself in the
midst of the refiner's fire. I
pray I can be strong enough
to understand that "tribulation
for righteousness is not a blessing
only, but also a gift that God giveth
unto none save his special friends."
(William Tyndale). Should I ever be
asked to lay my life on the holy altar
of sacrifice, I hope that I will have
the encouragement of faith, and
the comfort of His promise
that He will never leave
me nor forsake me.
(See Hebrews 13:5).

July 10

As I think about my Savior,

I come to the
epiphany that my
paltry possessions have
absolutely no bearing
on my capacity for
happiness.

Without the guidance of
inspiration from above, it is nigh
unto impossible to discover how to find real
happiness. Throughout history, both poverty and
wealth have failed miserably. It looks like neither fame
nor anonymity holds the key. Principalities and a lack of
worldly influence seem to be inadequate. It appears that
neither beauty nor the beast has the advantage. Joseph
Smith taught that happiness has very little to do with
things that can be quantified. He explained that it
is ordained of God that "happiness is the object
and design of our existence," but that it will
only "be the end thereof if we pursue the
path that leads to it; and this path is
virtue, uprightness, faithfulness,
holiness, and keeping all the
commandments of God."

July 11

As I think about my Savior,

I
remember my
other role models; my
father, mother, teachers,
mentors, bishops, home
teachers, co-workers,
and friends and
neighbors.

All of
them have
strengthened
my testimony and
nurtured my struggling
spirit so that I might have a
more sure witness of the Savior.
Sir Isaac Newton invented calculus,
defined the laws of motion, and has
been credited with an astounding
list of other accomplishments.
Asked how he was able to do
it all, he simply replied: "I
stood on the shoulders
of giants."

July 12

As I think about my Savior,

it
dawns on
me, and were
it not for my faith
would be extremely
unsettling, that the
adversary also
knows me by
name.

Satan often uses
private contractors, who are
nothing more than vipers, whose
sole purpose as they slither about in the
shadows is to destroy faith, particularly of those
who are in a covenant relationship with the Lord. The
powerful antidotes to the telestial trauma caused by the
venom of the snakebites of Satan's sidekicks are recurring
repentance, the safety of the sacrament, and celestial
service, for those who lose their lives in Christ shall
find them again. I cannot hope to lift others up
out of the jungle in which these serpents
hide, unless I am standing firmly
on higher ground.

July 13

As I think about my Savior,

I am
inspired by His
unselfish example
to be quick to share
the gifts of my time,
talents, and means
with others.

The Savior
encouraged his disciples
to focus their attention on their
less fortunate brethren and to lose
themselves in service. He knew that by
doing so they would eventually be brought
into complete harmony with the attributes of
their Father in Heaven. By conforming their lives
to these divine character traits, their very nature
would be transformed as they assumed not only
the image, but also the likeness of God. They
would be of one mind and purpose. "And
ye shall be even as I am," he explained,
"and I am even as the Father, and
the Father and I are one."
(3 Nephi 28:10).

July 14

As I think about my Savior,

and
listen,
I can hear
Him calling
me from a
land of
woe.

We are
now beginning
to witness the recurring
spectacle of Babylon crumbling
into the dust, as Heavenly Father
overthrows her mighty towers. Force
and compulsion have failed miserably, as
they have tried to establish an ideal society.
His battle plan, on the other hand, addresses
the transformation of individual souls, one
by one, as they are redeemed from sin
and inspired to righteously exercise
their agency, to live in complete
harmony with the Great
Plan of the Eternal
God.

July 15

As I think about my Savior,

and see how His
ministry has caused
a great division among
the people, I am ever
more grateful for
my testimony.

In the Last Days, mortal
combatants with increasingly
polarized viewpoints have rekindled
the ideological War in Heaven, by once
again positioning themselves within camps
that are diametrically opposed to each other.
Champions of righteousness use the word of
the Lord as a weapon that is sharper than a
two-edged sword, and that divides truth
from error, penetrating to the innermost
parts, and separating the sheep from
the goats and the wheat from the
tares. Emissaries of Satan use
words as well, but only to
deceive the children of
men and lead them
astray.

July 16

As I think about my Savior

and His doctrine, I know that He will anticipate my needs and speak directly to my spirit.

Every principle of the Gospel carries within itself its own independent witness that it is true. The Lord delights in clarity, and "he speaketh unto men according to their language, unto their understanding." (2 Nephi 31:3). Communication via the Spirit is universally understood by those who have paid the price to develop fluency in that celestial tongue. The miracle is that as spiritual rapport with the heavens confirms our faith, scales of darkness fall from our eyes and vistas of eternal proportion are opened to our view.

July 17

As I think about my Savior,

I will find
the courage to
bear my afflictions
with long-suffering,
even if they are
unmerited.

"For what
praise is it, when
ye be buffeted for your
faults, ye take it patiently?
But when ye do well, and ye
suffer wrong and take it patiently,
then is there thanks with God. Hereunto
verily were ye called." (William Tyndale).
"Blessed are ye when men shall revile you and
persecute, and shall say all manner of evil against
you falsely, for my sake, for ye shall have great
joy and be exceedingly glad, for great shall be
your reward in heaven; for so persecuted
they the prophets who were before you."
(3 Nephi 12:11-12). At the end of the
day, "we can never be injured by
any mortals except ourselves."
(Heber J. Grant).

July 18

As I think about my Savior,

He
gives me
a swift kick in
my status quo, to
jump-start my
real journey
home.

As I advance in
years, and become more
aware of the ephemeral nature of
my mortality, I sometimes find myself
thinking of stepping on shore, and finding
that it is heaven, of taking hold of a hand, and
finding that it is God's, of breathing a new air,
and experiencing celestial aether for the first
time, of feeling invigorated, and realizing
that it is immortality, of passing from the
tempests of the telestial world to the
unbroken calm of God's Rest, of
waking up as if from a dream,
and finding that I have
come full circle and
am back home.

July 19

As I think about my Savior

even as I interact
with the wicked, I try a little
harder to "overcome evil with
good; that is, with all softness,
kindness, and all patience win
him, even as God with
kindness" won me.
(William Tyndale).

If the
advancing
tide of evil is ever
to be contained, I must first
remember that it is far better to
hold up a candle than it is to curse
the darkness. If, together, we can muster
that kind of courage, we will stem the surge
of a satanic effluent. A thousand points of light,
when taken together, cast a very long shadow.
Abraham Lincoln said that to sin by silence,
when words should be spoken, makes
cowards of men. That warning
has never been more
timely.

July 20

As I think about my Savior,

faith in
my soul's
immortality is
affirmed, because
within myself I can
feel the relentless
tug of immortal
longings.

The poet both asked and answered my questions: "Who are these children coming down like gentle rain through darkened skies, with glory trailing from their feet as they go, and endless promise in their eyes? Who are these young ones growing tall, growing strong, like silver trees against the storm; who will not bend with the wind or the change, but stand to fight the world alone? These are the few, the warriors saved for Saturday; to come the last day of the world. These are the strong, the warriors rising in their might to win the battle raging in the hearts of men, on Saturday."
(Doug Stewart).

July 21

As I think about my Savior,

and I
find myself
being drawn into
a tangible immersion
in the pure and refining
element of the Spirit, I
breach the boundary
of time itself, into
the crucible in
which we
burn.

It
may be
that I am
"a stranger in
a strange land,"
(Exodus 2:22), and
will never be entirely
comfortable as a mortal,
or at home in time, for I
more properly belong
to the eternities.

July 22

As I think about my Savior,

my
well-considered
dreams define my
destiny, while those
that are but whimsical
desires will evaporate
like the dew before
the face of the
morning
sun.

"Why is it,"
asked the poet,
that whenever I reach
for the sky to climb aboard
cloud nine, it evaporates and rains
upon my dreams? Is it a matter of science,
or simply a matter of fact, that not even a cloud
with a silver lining can hold the weight of our
dreams without some precipitation? I think
I've found the answer to this dilemma.
Keep on reaching for the sky, but
don't forget your umbrella."
(Susan Stephenson).

July 23

As I think about my Savior,

I cherish
my relationship
with Him Who
is my Elder
Brother.

We know
from His description in
the scriptures that Jesus was
a man who generated enthusiasm
in His disciples; who instilled confidence
in their hearts; who showed how to fix mistakes
rather than to assign blame. He was unmistakably
certain of His authority, but nevertheless delegated
responsibility; undeniably He knew how, but more
often than not, He showed how. He never reduced
work to drudgery, but instead elevated it to both
excitement and enjoyment. Instead of focusing
on the concentration of power, He generated
co-operation. He never drove His disciples
forward, but was always out in front of
them, leading them along paths of
righteousness to still waters
and green pastures.

July 24

As I think about my Savior,

I am thankful
for the opportunities
I am given to recover my
composure, reprioritize my
objectives, and rededicate
my efforts, in order to
restore the alignment
of my behavior with
His vision of my
potential.

Unlike an
indulgent parent,
my Father in Heaven
will not dote upon me, give
me that which I do not deserve, or
submit to my insistent petitions to
give me that which I do not need.
Nevertheless, He has promised a
great endowment and blessing
to be poured out upon me,
if only I remain faithful
and continue to walk
in humility.

July 25

As I think about my Savior,

I sense the
sparkle in His
eyes, that can only
be a reflection of His
unbridled optimism
in my capacity to
make correct
choices.

I
realize that
"fame is a vapor, and
popularity is an accident,"
and that "those who cheer you
today may curse you tomorrow. In
the end, the only thing that endures
is character." (Horace Greeley). I see
the four cardinal virtues of patience,
justice, fortitude, and temperance
in every babe who has joined the
human family, for we are all
the children of God, who
have inherited His
qualities.

July 26

As I think about my Savior,

my timid
prayers are as a
venturing kite that
reaches out above
the chasm of fear
all the way to
heaven.

In the prototypical
Lord's prayer, Jesus Christ implied
that His Father is in a place where Satan can
never trespass. His dwelling is completely secure;
it is a sea of glass, a Urim and Thummim, a place of
brilliant transparency, lucidity, purity, inspiration, and
revelation. For me, it is a secret garden where I can go in
my prayers to be with Him, but it is also where I will go
to live with Him forever. His existence is undeniable.
In Him there is "no variableness, neither shadow of
turning." (James 1:17). It is my faith and testimony
that, once and for all, He will banish ignorance
and eliminate ambiguity by creating clarity
in a flood of unimaginably intense and
unearthly Son-light that will envelop
the earth in its warm embrace.

July 27

As I think about my Savior,

I realize
that He is the
rudder of my
ship, my sextant,
and my compass,
with the power
to orient me
toward the
eternities.

A good mariner is able
to read the weather like a book,
and can focus his nautical skills to trim
his sails and set a course that will unerringly
lead him to a safe harbor. The very same wind
that might cause a less seaworthy craft to founder
will fill the sails of the vessel of a skilled seaman. The
helmsman may not necessarily see the port of call that is
his destination. Sometimes, it is beyond the horizon,
and sometimes the tack of the vessel appears to be
taking the ship away from its objective. But if
correct principles are followed, even in
the face of steady headwinds, the
landfall is always sure.

July 27

As I think about my Savior,

I
resolve to
throw open
my shutters,
and unbolt my
door, that even
strangers might
be welcomed to
my hearth and
home, without
regard to who
they might
be.

The Pharisees were critical of the Lord's association with the wrong crowd, consisting of publicans and sinners, but He explained: "They that be whole need not a physician, but they that are sick… I am not come to call the righteous but sinners to repentance." (Matthew 9:12-13).

July 28

As I think about my Savior,

I can
see that
the Gospel
is "the Good
News" to all
those who
embrace
it.

The
Word provides
every one of the principles,
ordinances, and covenants that
are necessary for me to become sanctified
so that I may become worthy to live once again
in a state of holiness in the presence of my Heavenly
Father. Because of the Gospel, I may come unto Christ,
where I may "lay hold upon every good gift...and be
perfected in him." (Moroni 10:32). If I "continue in
the supplication of his grace," it will be my
privilege to stand blameless before
Him when I meet Him at
His pleasing bar.
(Alma 7:3).

July 29

As I think about my Savior,

it is
my conviction
that the dark clouds of
error will be dispelled as they
evaporate before the brilliant
rays of divine truth that
are the distinguishing
characteristics of the
Restoration of
His Gospel.

I will
not be ashamed to
"declare his doing among
the people." Fearlessly and
convincingly, I will yoke myself
with those who "make mention that
His name is exalted." (2 Nephi 22:4). I
will link arms with my brethren who
have made the decision to "stand as
witnesses of God at all times and
in all things, and in all places
…even until death."
(Mosiah 18:9).

July 30

As I think about my Savior,

I realize
that I must
make a more
concerted effort
to "progress to an
endless advancement
in eternal perfections."
(Brigham Young).

Thus,
as I seek to
better myself, I will
remember that if I always
do what I always did, I'll always
get what I always got. Even if I'm on
the right road, I'm going to get run over
if I just sit there smelling the flowers. As I
seek improvement, my ideals will be as stars.
"I will not succeed in touching them with my
hands. But, like the seafaring man in the
desert of waters, if I choose them as
my guides and follow them, I
will reach my destiny."
(Carl Shurz).

July 31

As I think about my Savior

if I
disregard life's
trivialities, but only
concentrate my attention
on the sweeping panorama
of our Father's Plan, it will
intuitively all begin
to make sense.

The glittering facets
of the life of the Spirit allow
me to see beyond the limited horizon
of my natural vision. When John Widtsoe
traveled to England, the immigration official who
interviewed him, asked: "If I were to allow you to enter
Britain, what would you teach our people?" Elder Witdsoe
said: "I would teach them where they came from, why they
are here, and where they are going." The official looked
at him and asked: "Does your church teach that?" His
voice brimming with a confidence born of faith,
Elder Witdsoe declared: "It does." "Well mine
doesn't," the official responded, and he
stamped his passport, signed it, and
said: "You may enter!"

"Blessed are they which are persecuted
for righteousness' sake: for theirs
is the kingdom of heaven."
(Matthew 5:10).

August 1

As I think about my Savior,

I silently
plead with Him to
fight my battles for
me, to stay close by
me, to watch over
me and to never
forsake me, and
to love me
forever.

Amidst the yin and
the yang of my temporal
education, if I have failed to do
the same for others, I have made
the implicit confession that I never
really knew Him, and that for me He
lived and died in vain. It also suggests
that His teachings meant nothing to me,
and that in my thoughts and deeds I
never drew near enough to Him to
allow myself to be mesmerized
by His mercy, and to fall
under the spell of His
compassion.

August 2

As I think about my Savior

as I twist and
turn to avoid the
telestial tackles that
are part of the game of
life, I grow more aware
of His influence over each
participant in the contest.
I am in awe of His skill
as my personal trainer
and my defensive
coordinator.

In
the midst of
adversity, William
Tyndale confidently
wrote from prison that
"this knowledge declares
that we are safe already,
and certifies our hearts
and makes us feel that
our faith is right and
that God's spirit
is in us."

August 3

As I think about my Savior,

I enjoy
a heightened
sense of the soul
stirring realities that
swirl all around me, that
speak directly to my spirit
because they are illuminated
by a penetrating spotlight
from above that receives
its power from the
Holy Ghost.

Too
often, we are
"clever, interesting,
and brilliant, but we lack
one of the three dimensions
of life. We have no upward reach.
Our conversation sparkles, but it
is frivolous and often flippant.
Our talk is witty, but is often
at the expense of high
and sacred things."
(Charles Jefferson).

August 4

As I think about my Savior,

the
feeling
will kindle
within my heart
a faith that will burn
ever more brightly,
that I might walk
with confidence
in the light
of truth.

As I do so, my heart
will cry out: "I love thee, Lord
Jesus, look down from the sky, and
stay by my cradle, till morning is nigh." (Text
attr. to Martin Luther). Reflecting my own hopes
and fears of all the years, the poet said "to the man
who stood at the gate of the year, 'Give me a light
that I may tread safely into the unknown.' And
the man replied: 'Go forth in the darkness
and put your hand into the hand of God,
which shall be to you better than a
light and safer than the known
way.'" (Minnie Haskins).

August 5

As I think about my Savior,

I gather the gold dust of
time, and cash it in, in order to
purchase moments of reflection
that allow me to ponder the
meaning and purpose
of my life.

I
pause to
consider how silently
the wondrous gift has been
given; that our Heavenly Father
has imparted to human hearts the
blessings of heaven. I realize that "life is
a sheet of paper white, where each of us
may write a line or two, and then comes
night. Greatly begin. If thou hast time
but for a line, make that sublime." It
is "not failure, but low aim" that
"is crime." (James Lowell). The
Lord encourages me to raise
my sights, and to
aim for the
stars.

August 6

As I think about my Savior,

I am given a
reprieve from my
relentless pursuit of
traumatizing trinkets,
temporal treasures,
telestial trivialities,
and territorial
triflings.

As I stretch
my spiritual muscles
and brush the cobwebs from
my clouded mind, I crane my neck
to see beyond heaven's gate. Thus, is set
in motion a contest between my hard-hearted
and stiff-necked carnal nature, and a perspective that
gives me pliancy and perspective, and introduces me to the
companionship of the Holy Ghost "which maketh manifest
unto the children of men, according to their faith." (Jarom
1:4). I begin to realize that it is my spiritual inflexibility
that has been preventing me from looking up to my
Heavenly Father for guidance, over to priesthood
leaders for counsel, around to seek out those
in need, or down in an attitude of humility.

August 7

As I think about my Savior,

my testimony is strengthened as I realize that every heavenly truth carries within itself its own witness that requires no external warrant.

The Savior created a missionary moment to teach a powerful truth, when He said: "Let your light so shine before this people that they may see your good works and glorify your Father Who is in heaven." He surely meant that He should be reflected in all that I do, so that when others would see my good works, their thoughts would turn to Him. (Matthew 5:16). For to Him belongs the power and the glory, and I am unworthy to unloose even the latchets of His shoes.

August 8

As I think about my Savior,

I look to the
experiences of
others, and to the
lessons of religious
history, to give me
vitally needed
perspectives
on life.

The poet
observed: "The
past is prologue,"
but history does not
necessarily have to repeat
itself. We are not caught in a
time-warp, doomed to play over
and over again the mistakes of our
forbearers. What a wonderful blessing
it is to be able to study the messages of the
scriptures, and then to incorporate into our
lives unchanging principles of eternal life,
thereby to avoid the doctrinal detours,
the conceptual quicksands, and the
perceptual pitfalls of the past.

August 9

As I think about my Savior,

I am
struck by the
realization that
my journey through
mortality could very well
lead to my own personally
tailored Gethsemane
experience.

All of us
must follow the
same course whether
we be rich or poor, educated
or untrained, tall or short, prince
or pauper, king or commoner. There
is only one way. "It is a long road
spiked with thorns and briars
and pitfalls and problems."
(Spencer W. Kimball).
But it is the only
path that leads
back to our
heavenly
home.

August 10

As I think about my Savior,

He becomes a
spiritual chaperone
Whose guidance helps
me to avoid distractions
that could detour me onto
telestial tangents, even as
I seek after "wisdom
and great treasures
of knowledge."
(D&C 89:19).

The process
of inquiry demands
my thorough search for
those pearls that may not be
readily discernable after only a
cursory glance. I must take care
how I handle the oracles of God,
"lest they are accounted as a light
thing, (and I am) brought under
condemnation thereby, and
stumble and fall when the
storms descend."
(D&C 90:5).

August 11

As I think about my Savior,

I am
transported
into everlasting
burnings, where my
heart begins to melt in
the fervent heat of
the fiery furnace
of my faith.

As
I meditate
upon the love of
my Redeemer, "glories
stream from heaven afar,
(with) heavenly hosts singing
alleluia!" (Franz Gruber). Sweet
symphonies penetrate my rough
exterior to touch my soul and
resonate in perfect harmony
with my heart strings, so
much so that my spirit
comes alive, and I am
motivated to join
the choir.

August 12

As I think about my Savior,

I know that
when my eyes at
last shall see Him,
the miracle will have
been made possible only
because He provided
a Plan, that I might
experience His
redeeming
love.

With His prophet, I know
that in a coming day, "I shall
feel the nail marks in His hands and
in His feet, and shall wet His feet with
my tears. But I shall not know any better
then, than I know now, that He is God's
Almighty Son, that He is our Savior and
Redeemer, and that salvation comes
in and through His atoning blood
and in no other way." (The last
testimony of Elder Bruce
R. McConkie).

August 13

As I think about my Savior,

I recall how effectively He taught by precept, as well as by example, that an ounce of help is almost always better than a pound of preaching.

"We have paused on some plateaus long enough. Let us resume our journey forward and upward, and quietly put an end to our reluctance to reach out to others, whether in our own families, wards, or neighborhoods. We have been diverted at times from fundamentals on which we must now focus, in order to move forward as a person or as a people." (Spencer W. Kimball). As Gordon B. Hinckley re-affirmed: "The Church cannot hope to save a man on Sunday, if during the week it is a complacent witness to the destruction of his soul."

August 14

As I think about my Savior,

the
Spirit quietly
confirms that Christ
dependency is more
important than my
misguided craving
for self sufficiency
could ever
be.

I realize that His teachings are intended to change my nature so that I may progress to the point where I reflect His attributes in perfection. The uncorrupted behavior to which I aspire will reflect my love of all mankind. The righteous exercise of agency that is my quest will be mirrored in my discipline. The comprehension of His omniscience and His omnipotence, that I desire, will be reflected in my appreciation for God's Great and Merciful Plan, and in my gratitude for Christ's compassion, His atoning sacrifice, and my hope of a glorious resurrection.

August 15

As I think about my Savior,

the melodic
composition of the
Gospel, punctuated
by an animated pattern
of the satisfying strains
of His redeeming love,
resonates within my
heart and provides
the tempo for its
steady beat.

It is my hope
to receive God's love that
will lead me to repentance and
then to mercy and forgiveness through
the Atonement of our Savior Jesus Christ. I
hope to be transformed as I learn to submit to
His will and develop His character and nature.
I will rely upon His promise: "All that I have,
I could give to you, but what I am, you
must earn for yourself, line upon line
and precept upon precept."
(See Isaiah 28:10).

August 16

As I think about my Savior,

I realize
that even as I am
drawn to Him today,
I trace the footsteps of
those who followed His
star from the East
so long ago.

Heber J.
Grant said that
we are truly wise when
"we are striving, working,
trying to the best of our ability to
improve day by day." Then, he said
"we are in the line of our duty if we are
seeking to remedy our own defects, if we
are so living that we can ask for light, for
knowledge, for intelligence, and above
all, for His Spirit so that we may
overcome weakness. Then, I
can tell you, we are in the
straight and narrow
path that leads to
life eternal."

August 17

As I think about my Savior,

I am
filled with
faith as if
it were a
living
fire.

"I will rest
in the shade of trees,
and I will drink from the
cooling fountains. I will abide
in places of refuge from the storm.
I will mount up as on eagles' wings,
and I will be lifted out of an insane and
evil world. I will be as fair as the sun and
clear as the moon. My children will bow
down at His feet and worship Him as
the Lord of Lords and the King of
Kings. They will bathe His feet
with their tears and He will
weep and bless them."
(Vaughn Featherstone).

August 18

As I think about my Savior,

I
feel the
surge of an
upward reach
that persistently
tugs at my soul,
and requires
my reply.

When the
spirit that dwells
within my mortal clay has
been positively charged with the
energy of His influence, I will tingle with
excitement as the Holy Ghost animates every
fiber of my being. A pulsing witness of truth that
can only come from above demands that I no longer
remain passive. I cannot allow myself to continue to be
unresponsive to the good news found in the Gospel.
As Parley P. Pratt unflinchingly declared: "I have
received the holy anointing, and I can never
rest until the last enemy is conquered,
death is destroyed, and the truth
reigns triumphant."

August 19

As I think about my Savior,

I surrender to Him my
agency to act independently,
but it is in that very process that my
telestial tendencies become celestial
sureties; I sacrifice my free will
to release the blessings of
heaven in my behalf.
(See Malachi 3:10).

The Son of the
Living God is the
tangible and effectual
bridge between the secular
on the one hand and the sacred
on the other. Our autonomy may be
exhilarating, but its greatest expression
comes when we finally realize that, for our
own good, we must yield our undisciplined
will to His better judgment. He has enjoined
us over 900 times in the scriptures: "Come
unto me," because only in Him can "we
live, and move, and have our being."
There simply is no other way.
(Acts 17:28).

August 20

As I think about my Savior,

and I study the
New Testament and Book
of Mormon Gospels, I realize
that all scripture may be
"expounded…in one."
(3 Nephi 23:14).

The words of
eternal life "shall
be one in thine hand."
(Ezekiel 37:27). It matters
very little whether our religious
education has come from biblical
teachings or from Book of Mormon
instruction, in commandments from
the Doctrine & Covenants, or by way
of exhortation from the pages of the
Pearl of Great Price. If we receive
it from pulpits that are aflame
with faith, it is the same. The
word of God must always
be established in the
mouths of two or
three credible
witnesses.

August 21

As I think about my Savior,

I appreciate the harmony that exists between my stewardship responsibilities and my solemn covenant of consecration.

John K. Edmunds, who also served as the President of the Salt Lake Temple, enjoyed a long and distinguished legal career in Chicago. One day, a widow came to him for advice, and when they were finished, she apprehensively asked: "How much do I owe you?" Gently, he responded, "Why don't you pay me what you think it's worth. Greatly relieved, she got out her coin purse, fished around for a quarter, and pressed it into his hand. He looked at the quarter, looked at her, and then got out his own coin purse, and gave her ten cents change.

August 22

As I think about my Savior,

I hope to set
myself apart, and to be
"distinguished for (my) zeal
towards God, and also
towards men."
(Alma 27:27).

True
disciples of Christ
are honest, decent, noble,
respected, principled, and
firm in the faith. "God, give us
men!" urged Josiah Holland, well
over a century ago. "A time like this
demands strong minds, great hearts, true
faith and ready hands; men whom the lust
of office does not kill; men whom the spoils of
office cannot buy; men who possess opinions
and a will; men who have honor; men who
will not lie; men who can stand before a
demagogue and damn his treacherous
flatteries without winking! Tall sun-
crowned men, who live above
the fog in public duty and
in private thinking."

August 23

As I think about my Savior,

He extends to
me the open invitation to
partake of fountains of living
water, when I thirst; to come
and "buy wine and milk
without money and
without price."
(Isaiah 55:1).

The Spirit leads me to
believe Isaiah's promise that,
without reservation, the invitation to
enjoy eternal possibilities will be extended
to all of God's children. Helen Keller clearly
understood "there is one tragedy in life that is
worse than to be born without sight, and that
is to be born with sight, but without vision."
She asked: "Why cannot the soul go forth
from its dwelling place and, discarding
the poor lenses of the body, peer
through the telescope of truth
into the infinite reaches
of immortality?"

August 24

As I think about my Savior,

He ratifies
my supposition
that sin is
waste.

I am behaving
sinfully when I follow
one course of action, when
something of far greater value
could have been done instead. I am
sinful whenever I settle for mediocrity
instead of buckling down and pursuing a
difficult road that climbs to greater heights
with superb views of the way that lies before.
Sin is my capitulation to a spiritual stagnation
instead of my eager acceptance of the rewards
related to eternal progression. It is trading a
mess of pottage for an eternal birthright. It
is nothing more than an overnight stay in
a second-class hotel, while on the other
side of town is a five star all-inclusive
property with no resort amenities
fee, and plenty of room for me
on the highest floor, in its
penthouse suite.

August 25

As I think about my Savior,

I am
able to bridge the
exasperating gulf that can
exist between heaven and earth,
and make the quantum leap
from the world of every
day all the way to
eternity.

It is an
exciting time to be
alive, because "in the Last
Days, our discipleship will be
lived in crescendo." (Neal Maxwell).
As soon as I fall in step with the cadence
of the Gospel, my increasing pulse rate will
quickly confirm that the blessings that follow
obedience have a performance cost. Hence,
the revelatory avowal of Brigham Young:
"I never count the cost of anything," he
said." I just find out what the Lord
wants me to do, and I do it." We
need to do it, do it right, and
do it right now.

August 26

As I think about my Savior,

and ask
a blessing
on the food in
the company of
my loved ones at
mealtime, I visualize
another gathering in
the not too distant
future, to which
I have already
been invited.

My personalized
summons to that gustatory
celebration has already been
extended, and the items on the
menu have been finalized. At that
splendid "banquet of consequences,
there will not be much that is satisfying
at the table unless I am able to bow my
head in reverence, rather than hang
it in shame, in the presence of
God, Who will be there."
(Marion D. Hanks).

August 27

As I think about my Savior,

I
eagerly
anticipate
another chance
to slake my thirst
by drawing freely
from His fountain
of living water.

If I consciously elect to
deny myself the satisfaction of
the spiritual fortification that can be
provided by the Word of God, my own
portion must inevitably diminish further
and further, until I find myself defenseless
against the aggressive tactics of the devil. If
I am left to my own devices, I will slowly die
of thirst in the barren desert of Babylon. I will
be influenced more by the deceiver's lies than
by the illuminating truths of the Spirit. With
a parched throat and cracked lips, I will be
unable to muster so much as a hoarse cry
of protest, as I am dragged from the dry
lakebed of Lucifer straight to hell.

August 28

As I think about my Savior,

I am
prompted to
exhibit generosity
and to extend my love
to those who, through
no fault of their own,
are in less fortunate
circumstances
than I.

Before Fiorello
La Guardia became
the mayor of New York City,
he was a magistrate. One day there
appeared before him a man accused of
stealing a loaf of bread. Upon questioning,
the man explained that he'd committed
the crime to feed his starving family.
Whereupon, La Guardia dismissed
the case, and sentenced all in the
courtroom to pay a fine for
living in a city where a
man had to steal to
feed his family.

August 29

As I think about my Savior,

and realize
that we are all
beggars who will
forever be in His debt,
I am moved to extend
charity, or the pure
love of Christ, to
those around
me.

"When thou hurtest
not thy neighbours, then
art thou sure that God's Spirit
worketh in thee and that thy faith
is no dream nor any false imagination."
(William Tyndale). "Blessed are the merciful,"
the Savior taught, "for they shall obtain mercy."
(3 Nephi 12:7). "For with what judgment ye judge,
ye shall be judged: and with what measure ye mete,
it shall be measured to you again." (Matthew 7:2).
What goes around, comes around, and if I cast
my bread upon the waters, I can be sure that
after many days, it shall return to me.
(See Ecclesiastes 11:1).

August 30

As I think about my Savior,

He
infuses me
with the courage
to confront, as well as
the power to engage, all
those who would try to
sabotage my petitions
by secularizing
the sacred.

I remember well the
account in the scriptures that
describes how the Savior scattered
the tables of the moneychangers at the
temple in Jerusalem. How cheaply do we sell
that which is most dear to us. "That for which
all virtue is sold, and almost any vice – almighty
gold!" (Ben Jonson). How ironic that it is all for
nothing! The world's covetous passion to
hoard telestial trash leads to societal
bickering that can pave the way to
"the destruction of nearly all the
people of the kingdom."
(Ether 9:12).

August 31

As I think about my Savior,

the
spirit quietly
teaches me that
real poverty is my
untested potential, the
unintended casualty
of my limiting
beliefs.

He
gives me
weakness, that I
might learn to be humble
and to accept His grace. But He
also gives me His strength to meet my
challenges and to overcome adversity. As
I become more aware of my God-given talents,
I learn to focus my energies in constructive ways.
When I view myself in a partnership with God, and
I am infused not only with His energy, but also
with His optimism, potential stumbling blocks
become stepping stones that can only lead
me to greater heights of personal
achievement.

"Blessed are ye, when men shall revile you, and persecute you, and shall say all manner of evil against you falsely, for my sake."
(Matthew 5:11).

September 1

As I think about my Savior,

I
realize
that even a
wretched soul
such as mine still
has access to
the intimate
comfort of
prayer.

The
touching story is told of
two friends at the Auschwitz
Concentration Camp, during World
War Two. One felt completely alone and
forgotten, his situation hopeless. The other
knelt down each morning to pray, and his
companion finally berated him for it. "For
what could you possibly thank God,
given our terrible circumstances?"
he asked. His friend quietly
replied, "Every day, I
thank God that I am
not like them."

September 2

As I think about my Savior,

I hope
that I will be less
likely to break the tenth
commandment by coveting
the profane treasures of the
earth, or the gods of wood
and stone envisioned
by the prophets.
(See Isaiah 37:19).

These are only
counterfeit pleasures that
are but the poor substitutes for the
blessing of happiness that God reserves
for the faithful. Undisciplined minds are easily
swayed by the siren song so seductively sent by Satan.
Unprincipled character will crumble in the face of telestial
temptations that are so tantalizing and yet so traumatizing.
However, the more our society focuses on the idols of the
day, the less prevalent is the legitimate rule of those
who bear the priesthood. In the sight of God, this
substitution of the sacred by the profane is an
abomination, for idol worship can be the
epitome of taking His name in vain.

September 3

As I think about my Savior,

He is able to free
me to look beyond my
perceived limitations, Satan's
imitations, the world's obfuscations,
false priests' ministrations, and my
worst critics' prognostications, so
that I may more clearly see the
footings and the foundations
that underpin the exhibition
of the full stature of
my spirit.

The indomitable
Helen Keller, who triumphed
over the silence and darkness in her
life, wrote that "faith, the spiritual strong
searchlight, illuminates the way, and although
sinister doubts lurk in the shadow, I walk unafraid
towards the Enchanted Wood where the foliage
is always green, where joy abides, where
nightingales nest and sing, and where
life and death are one in the
presence of the Lord."
("Midstream").

September 4

As I think about my Savior,

and
ponder
the humble
circumstances
that surrounded His
birth and ministry, I am
able to see more clearly
where I should place
my own priorities.

Our
Heavenly Father
abases the wealthy that the
poor might be exalted. Babylon
worships before the throne of the
almighty dollar, patronizes propriety,
glories in the adoration of the treasures
of the earth, deals in counterfeit currency,
destroys initiative through a misguided sense
of entitlement, allows blind ambition to replace
righteous desire, and suppresses upward
mobility and progress by maintaining
the status-quo at the expense of
drive and determination.

September 5

As I think about my Savior,

I put in its proper
perspective my preparation
that is unfaltering, unrelenting,
unflagging, untiring, and
unmitigated, as much
as it is purposeful
and persistently
prayerful.

"This life,
(after all,) is
the time for (me)
to prepare to meet
(my) Maker; yea, behold
the day of this life is the day
for (me) to perform (my) labors,"
to heal through repentance the soul
scars of mortality, and attend to every
needful thing, in the anticipation of
my resurrection to glory and a
wonderful reunion with all
of my loved ones in the
Celestial Kingdom.
(Alma 34:32).

September 6

As I think about my Savior,

I
thank Him that
He has inspired His
prophets to record their
testimonies, that my faith
might thereby not only
be sustained, but also
strengthened should
it ever begin
to falter.

"I
shall speak
unto the Jews and
they shall write it; and
I shall also speak unto the
Nephites and they shall write it;
and I shall also speak unto the other
tribes of the house of Israel, which
I have led away, and they shall
write it; and I shall also speak
unto all nations of the earth
and they shall write it."
(2 Nephi 29:12).

September 7

As I think about my Savior,

I
find the
strength to be
firm, steadfast,
unflinching, and
immoveable, as
I stand up for
the right.

I
pray that I
might be faithful and
uncompromising when I
am faced with adversity, and
yet be as humble and tender as
a child; that I might be self-effacing,
and embarrassed to be held up as a role
model; that I might be sensitive to the
whisperings of the Spirit, and that I
might exert a positive influence
upon others as they deepen
their own testimonies of
His divinity and of
His Gospel.

September 8

As I think about my Savior,

I
feel the
supportive
presence of
the Holy
Spirit.

As
Lorenzo
Snow said of his
baptism of the Spirit:
"It was a tangible immersion
in the heavenly principle or element,
the Holy Ghost; and even more real and
physical in its effects upon every part of my
system than the immersion by water, dispelling
forever, so long as reason and memory last, all
possibility of doubt or fear in relation to the
fact that the Babe of Bethlehem is truly the
Son of God; also the fact that He is now
being revealed to the children of men,
and communicating knowledge,
the same as in the time
of the Apostles."

September 9

As I think about my Savior,

I consider the
lesson He taught His
disciples with nothing more
than seven loaves of bread, and
and "a few little fishes."
(Matthew 15:34).

As I think about the plenty
with which He has blessed me, I
ponder the sobering fact that, each year,
the average American family spends over
two thousand dollars dining out. A family
of 6 will have spent nearly three thousand
dollars, a ward, with 275 active members,
will have spent well over one hundred
thousand dollars, and a stake, with
3,000 members, will have spent
nearly one and a half million
dollars. This should be
food for thought, the
next time we see a
beggar with a
cardboard
sign.

September 10

As I think about my Savior,

I am
struck by the
realization that
"wickedness never
was happiness."
(Alma 41:10).

Each of
the laws of
God has been
perfectly crafted
with me in mind, to
have both a blessing and
a punishment affixed to it.
Obedience brings happiness,
while disobedience always ends
badly. "Despair cometh because
of iniquity," (Moroni 10:22),
and is the feeling of utter
hopelessness that is the
natural consequence
of the violation
of eternal
law.

September 11

As I think about my Savior,

I
strengthen my
resolve to follow
the path that
will lead me
back to His
kingdom.

The One
Whom we will all
meet before the gate of heaven
is the Lord Himself, for "he employeth
no servant there." (2 Nephi 9:41). As it was
for Alma and his people, so it will be for me. His
word will become my Liahona, and if I follow that
compass, I will find that no wind can blow except it
fills my sails. Although I may need to repetitively
tack during the voyage home, thereby pursuing
a course that seems to be taking me away from
my destination, and although I may stop at
any number of intriguing ports-of-call
along the way, I will always be
certain of my final
landfall.

September 12

As I think about my Savior,

I
express
gratitude that
the Word has been
revealed anew with
power, and with an
understanding that
is meant to be
universal.

There is
abroad in the land a
resource for guidance that is
more than inspiration, and can only
be described as revelation. It is essential
to vital religion, for it "cannot be maintained
and preserved on the theory that God dealt with
our human race only in the far past ages, and that
the Bible is the only evidence we have that our
God is living, revealing, and communicating.
If He ever spoke, God is still speaking.
He is the great I Am, and not
the great He Was."
(Rufus Jones).

September 13

As I think about my Savior,

I
pause to
reflect upon
my deep gratitude
to the mother of Jesus,
a pious young woman,
"a virgin espoused to a
man whose name
was Joseph."
(Luke 1:27).

Mary was a
chosen vessel of the Lord
who had found favor with God,
and who had obviously accepted her special
calling with profound sobriety. She would sacrifice
other opportunities for self-fulfillment, to instead nurture
her Son. As a writer once asked: "Are women who enjoy
motherhood today intellectual dropouts? What would
have become of the human race had Eve rejected
motherhood in favor of pursuing a more
gratifying career in the already
promising apple industry?"
("Time Magazine").

September 14

As I think about my Savior

I realize that
to forge lasting family
bonds, I need only look up
to discover in the heavens the
unmistakable evidence of eternal
life, and then to find a way to
hitch my wagon to the
star of Bethlehem.

That has always been
the formula. When he was
living in Rome at around the same
time as the birth of the Savior, the Stoic
philosopher Epictetus described our universe
as "but one great city, full of beloved ones, divine
and human, by nature endeared to each other." In
ways that defy description, "the mystic bond of
brotherhood makes all men one." (Thomas
Carlyle). In the end, "the brotherhood of
man is an integral part of Christianity
no less than the Fatherhood of God,
and to deny one is no less infidel
than to deny the other."
(Lyman Abbot).

September 15

As I think about my Savior,

and
especially as I
roll His teachings
over and over in my
mind and turn scriptural
statements into introspective
interrogatives, my ignorance of
doctrinal truth evaporates.

I have
learned to
trust in the Holy
Ghost to illuminate my
mind with answers, but only
if I have posed good questions.
When the Psalmist wrote: "Be still,
and know that I am God," he knew that
if I would be quiet and reflective, I would
experience spiritual symmetry and balance,
and that I would delight in a profound
comprehension of truth in response
to my heartfelt petitions.
(Psalms 46:10).

September 16

As I think about my Savior,

I
visualize a
wintery landscape
that has been softly
blanketed in white,
which I remember
is the symbol
of purity.

In language
that vividly recalls
the radiant countenances of
Moses and the prophet Abinadi,
(see Mosiah 13:5), Mormon recorded
of those to whom the Savior ministered,
that "they were as white as the countenance
and also the garments of Jesus; and behold the
whiteness thereof did exceed all the whiteness, yea,
even there could be nothing upon earth so white
as the whiteness thereof." (3 Nephi 19:25).
They had been washed clean and had
been sanctified in the redeeming
blood of Christ, and by His
grace had been saved.

September 17

As I think about my Savior,

I can
almost hear Him
extending to me the
invitation to come and
be perfected in Him,
and to deny myself
all ungodliness.
(See Moroni 10:32).

I am invited
by His Spirit to move
off the telestial turf that is Satan's
territorial treasure, and to seek instead
a place of sanctuary where the "covenants and
ordinances of God will fill me with faith as a living
fire. In a day of desolating sickness, scorched earth,
barren wastes, sickening plagues, disease, destruction,
and death, I will rest in the shade of trees and drink
from the cooling fountains. I will abide in a place
of refuge from the storm; mount up as upon the
wings of eagles and be lifted out of an insane
and evil world. I hope to be as fair as
the sun and clear as the moon."
(Vaughn Featherstone).

September 18

As I think about my Savior,

and realize
how many in the
world have despised
and rejected Him, I vow
that there will always
be room for Him
at my inn.

I must be careful to avoid
helping to build up the Church
while killing the articles of its faith,
or allowing its form to triumph over
spirit, because the Savior is counting on
my ardor and conviction. I cannot allow
myself to contribute to the expansion
of the assets of the kingdom, if the
cost is the loss of confidence in
the manifest destiny of latter-
day Zion. As the Church
grows institutionally,
I must do my part
to protect its
spiritual
core.

September 19

As I think about my Savior,

He fans the
flame of my resolve,
so that I might face my
timidity, step outside of
my comfort zone, and
introduce the Gospel
to others of His
children.

Because "salvation is not
a cheap experience," this may not
be easily accomplished. (Dallin Oaks).
Therefore, the Lord has revealed a strategic
battle plan for the Last Days, when His missionary
army will engage the forces of Babylon in mortal combat
by preaching the Gospel with power and authority. His
tactical objective is to banish ignorance, that all may
stand accountable for their own decisions. Because
the Lord has caused "a great division among the
people," we see the combatants forming into
ranks that have increasingly polarized
ideologies. (2 Nephi 30:10). Now
is the time to choose.
(See D&C 105:35).

September 20

As I think about my Savior,

and
embrace the
principles of His
Gospel, it is easier
for me to overcome
my preconceptions,
to reach out to those
with whom I would
ordinarily feel less
comfortable and
be less likely to
associate.

It was
with an
unflagging
positive mental
awareness that the
nephew of Ebenezer
Scrooge said: "I never
knew my mother. But I
hope to know Scrooge one
day." ("A Christmas Carol").

September 21

As I think about my Savior,

I
will make a
greater effort to
recognize the merits
of the principles of
His Plan, to honor
His law, and to
endure to the
end.

There
is a law that
has been irrevocably
decreed in heaven, that its
"powers cannot be handled or
controlled except upon the basis
of righteousness (which) cannot be
a superficial, ritualistic thing. It must
arise out of the deepest convictions of
the soul, not out of a desire merely
to 'go along' with the heavenly
crowd simply because that's
how things are done!"
(Neal Maxwell).

September 22

As I think about my Savior,

I realize I need to quicken
the pace of my journey
through mortality.

When I was
younger, I jogged every
morning through the Santa Monica
Mountains, above Pacific Palisades, in
Southern California. One day, as I neared
the end of my run, as I traced my way back
over the surface streets to my home, I stopped
at an intersection, waiting for the traffic signal to
change. I put my hands on my knees and with the
sweat dripping off the end of my nose, I thought
about aborting my run, stopping right then and
there, and allowing my complaining muscles
to cool down as I returned home. However,
through sweat-soaked eyes, I looked up,
and saw as it were, a vision before me.
Insistently flashing red with neon
brightness, directly in front of
me, were these words,
that urged me on:
"Don't walk!"

September 23

As I think about my Savior,

I better
understand and
more fully appreciate
the fathomless depths of
His Atonement, although
its full impact may not
hit me until I meet
Him at the Bar
of Justice.

"Hail the Sun of
Righteousness. Light and Life
to all He brings. Ris'n with healing
in His wings." (Charles Wesley). Within
the pages of The Book of Mormon, Another
Testament of Jesus Christ, we are clearly taught
that there can be "no other name given whereby
salvation cometh; therefore...take upon you the name
of Christ." (Mosiah 5:8). "Yea, come unto Christ, and be
perfected in him," taught Moroni, "and if ye shall deny
yourselves of all ungodliness, and love God with all
your might, mind, and strength, then is His grace
sufficient for you, that by His grace ye may
be perfect in Christ." (Moroni 10:32).

September 24

As I think about my Savior,

I
resolve
to try harder
than I have in
the past, to
honor Him
and serve
Him.

I can
stand taller,
walk straighter,
be more kind, speak
more gently, think more
carefully, give more freely,
act more responsibly, serve
more faithfully, listen more
attentively, receive more
graciously, laugh more
good-naturedly, cry
more tenderly and,
last of all, repent
even more
earnestly.

September 25

As I think about my Savior,

I am
moved to
refresh my
acquaintance
with Him, by
examining
His holy
word.

I will make time
in my busy life to be
contemplative, as I MapQuest
my way through the scriptures. For a
change, my study will not be a race. It will
not be necessary to blow through a prescribed
number of chapters or verses each day. Instead,
I will spend hours, if I like, while pondering a
single concept. I will turn it over and over
again in my mind, and cross-reference
it to other supportive teachings. It
will become my privilege to
obtain fresh perspectives
that will prove to be
enlightening.

September 26

As I think about my Savior,

and
meditate
upon His word,
I sense a harmony
with eternal principles
that is synchronous with
the rhythms in nature
that surround me
and resonate
with my
spirit.

The veil
isolating me from
the eternities is almost
transparent as I become more
sensitive. As my powers expand,
I experience the glittering facets of the
life of the Spirit. The Gospel sets me free
to be more creative, and encourages me
to push my limits, so that I may enjoy
greater freedom of expression and
redefine my potential. It is the
perfect law of liberty.

September 27

As I think about my Savior,

it strikes
me that He has
provided me with
unequaled opportunities
to carry the Gospel into the
world, sometimes without even
leaving the comfort of my own
home. "Reach out and touch
someone" has taken on a
whole new meaning
in cyberspace.

Too often, it is
the other way around,
and we bring worldliness
into the Gospel. We must not
tinker with the standards that the
Lord has established in His Church.
It is unthinkable that we would want
"to become popular with the world,"
said Ezra Taft Benson, "because
then all hell would want
to join us."

September 28

As I think about my Savior,

I
turn over
in my mind the
teaching moments
that surrounded His
ministry; as I do so,
I personalize them,
by applying them
to my own life
experiences.

"Not
enjoyment,
and not sorrow, is
our destined end or way;
but to act, that each tomorrow
finds us farther than today… Lives
of great men all remind us that we can
make our lives sublime, and departing,
leave behind us footprints on the sands of
time. Let us then be up and doing, with a
heart for any fate; still achieving, still
pursuing. Learn to labor, and to
wait." (Longfellow).

September 29

As I think about my Savior

and
all that
He did for
me, I realize
how puny, by
comparison, are
my timid attempts
to serve and to
sacrifice.

I have come to the
astounding conclusion
that there is really no-one
who ever made a sacrifice "for
the kingdom of heaven, except the
Savior. I would not give the ashes of a
rye straw for that man who feels that he
is making sacrifices for God. We are doing
this for our own happiness, welfare, and
exaltation, and for nobody else. What
we do, we do for the salvation of the
inhabitants of the earth, not for
the heavens, the angels, or
God." (Brigham Young).

September 30

As I think about my Savior,

I
commit
to move off
my status-quo
in order to make
positive lifestyle
changes.

The
real danger
in doing nothing is
that it is hard to know
when I have finished! My
good intentions may be noble,
but achievement is the hallmark
of progress. My power to abide by
rules that govern the game of life is
fueled by more than a couple of AA
batteries that may accompany the
manufacturer's instructions. It is
encouraged by my repetitively
righteous behavior that is the
foundation of my Christ-
centered lifestyle.

"Ye are the salt of the earth."
(Matthew 5:13).

October 1

As I think about my Savior,

and the
illumination
I enjoy as a result
of my membership
in the Church, I will
look forward to
receiving the
Sacrament
in a new
light.

"Partaking of its
emblems has not been
established as a specific means
of securing remission of sins, or for
any other special blessing, aside from
that of a continuing endowment of the
Holy Spirit." (James Talmage). The power
of the covenant underlying the ordinance
of the Sacrament, however, is enough
to shepherd us into the presence
of the Father, and of the Son,
and of the Holy Ghost.

October 2

As I think about my Savior,

His imprint upon my
soul encourages me to extend
the hand of fellowship to strangers,
to those whose bodies may be festooned
with piercings or tattoos, who may have a
different skin color, have unfamiliar customs,
speak another language, prepare unusual
foods, worship strange gods or even
idols, or favor offensive economic,
political, educational, or
social ideologies.

"And it
shall come to pass
that ye shall divide (the
land) by lot for an inheritance
unto you, and to the strangers that
sojourn among you, which shall beget
children among you; and they shall be unto
you as born in the country among the
children of Israel; they shall have
inheritance with you among
the tribes of Israel."
(Ezekiel 47:22)

October 3

As I think about my Savior,

I
review anew
my commitment to
internalize the principles
of the Gospel, and to execute
a plan of action that includes
the opportunity to regularly
give an accountability
report my labors.

My rapport with
the Savior will allow
me to more easily identify
and deal with the fingerprints
of Satan that are smeared all over
the idols with which he tempts me.
It is only my eternal perspective that
allows me to make a distinction between
happiness and its worldly counterfeits
that are the polarized opposites so
energetically promoted by the
enthusiastically ignorant
and blind leaders
of the blind.

October 4

As I think about my Savior,

the
Spirit
bears sweet
testimony that
it has taught me
"all that I must do,"
in order "to live with
Him some day."
(Naomi Randall).

I
will try to
put into practice the
counsel of John Taylor, who
taught: "There are some Christian
people in this world who, if a man were
poor or hungry, would say, 'Let us pray for
him.' I would suggest a little different regimen
for a person in this condition. Rather, take him
a bag of flour and a little beef or pork. A few
such comforts will do him more good than
your prayers." More often than not, an
ounce of help is far better than
a pound of preaching.

October 5

As I think about my Savior,

I
try to
listen with
my heart,
as well as
with my
ears.

Many of us
have experienced
times in our lives when
the gap between our secular
knowledge and sacred experiences
has simply been too wide to bridge with
profane language. For example, when Jesus
Christ spoke to His Father in the presence of the
Nephite Saints, "so great and marvelous were the
words which he prayed, that they cannot be written,
neither can they be uttered by man." (3 Nephi 19:34).
Nevertheless, the spiritual preparation of those who
were gathered permitted them to receive these
things, and so "they did understand in their
hearts the words which he prayed."
(2 Nephi 19:33).

October 6

As I think about my Savior,

I will
make the
commitment
to become more
fluent in the melodic
language of God's word,
and to rely more fully
upon the vehicles of
its expression.

Only after I have paid
the appropriate price, will the
teachings of the Lord and the recorded
testimonies of the prophets flow easily and
poetically to my mind. Fluency will come after
pondering individual verses, and after practice
that is manifested by memorization, recitation,
individual and cooperative study, comparison
with companion scriptures, expansion of my
understanding by the critical analysis of
supportive commentary from reliable
and authoritative sources, all
accompanied by fasting
and prayer.

October 7

As I think about my Savior,

I
make a
conscious
effort to turn
my attention
away from the
concerns of the
world, and hope
that they will lose
their appeal and
attraction for
me.

Often, I tend
to fill space, "as
if what I have, what I
am, is not enough. Being
affluent, I strangle myself
with what I can buy, things
whose opacity obstructs
my ability to see what
is really there."
(Gretel Erlich).

October 8

As I think about my Savior,

although
I may only
be taking baby
steps as I continue
my spiritual education,
they are, nevertheless,
pushing me forward
in the direction of
my dreams.

Alma
asked the people
of Zarahemla, "Have ye
spiritually been born of God?
Have ye received His image in your
countenances? Have ye experienced this
mighty change in your heart?" (Alma 5:14).
And then, the more penetrating question, posed
just a few verses later: "And now" my brothers
and sisters "if ye have experienced a change
of heart, and if ye have felt to sing the
song of redeeming love, I would
ask, can ye feel so now?
(Alma 5:26).

October 9

As I think about my Savior,

I
am
far more
inclined to
embrace the
teachable things
of the kingdom.

Joseph
Smith, who was
at the time a young man
himself, revealed a self-evident
truth relating to the youthful Jesus,
that speaks volumes: "He needed not
that any man should teach him." (J.S.T.
Matthew 3:25). It may be that we, too, are
"not born an empty tablet on which the chalk
of childhood writes. Maybe a child has swift,
untinctured affinity and response to his own
burning deeps." Perhaps "he has a whole,
happy, healthy relationship with the
core of creativity and spirituality
that is his glory-laden spirit."
(Truman Madsen).

October 10

As I think about my Savior,

if I
find that
my battery
is drained, and I
am out of power, I
know that I can always
receive a jump-start from His
limitless reserves of energy. He
is a Triple-A roadside service
provider. Access is Always
Available.

I pray
that the Gospel
will penetrate my heart,
heal my blindness and my
deafness, and ease the tension and
stiffness that too often characterize my
attitude, so much so that when I am dead,
others "will seek not my tomb in the earth,
but find it in the hearts of men." (Jalal
al Din al Rumi, the 14th century
Sufi poet who founded the
Order of Dervishes).

October 11

As I think about my Savior,

I realize
that the Law of
the Lord is "written
not with ink, but with
the Spirit of the living
God; not in tables of
stone, but in fleshy
tables of the heart.
(2 Corinthians 3:3).

"Blessed is the man
(whose) delight is in the
law of the Lord. (For) he shall
be like a tree planted by the rivers
of water, that bringeth forth his fruit in
his season; his leaf also shall not wither;
and whatsoever he doeth shall prosper. The
ungodly are not so: but are like the chaff which
the wind driveth away. Therefore, the ungodly
shall not stand in the judgment, nor sinners in
the congregation of the righteous. For the
Lord knoweth the way of the righteous:
but the way of the ungodly shall
perish." (Psalms 1:1-6).

October 12

As I think about my Savior,

I
realize
that, while
my gratitude is
related to my attitude,
it is inexorably linked
to my altitude.

"Gratitude is
not only the greatest
of virtues, but it is the parent
of all others." (Cicero). As I begin
to cultivate its feelings, a remarkable
transformation occurs, as good outweighs
evil, love overpowers jealousy, light drives
out darkness, knowledge overcomes ignorance,
humility overwhelms self-sufficiency, appreciation
banishes bitterness, courtesy incapacitates rudeness,
abundance supersedes poverty, and well-being
disables weakness. When I begin the day
with heartfelt expressions of gratitude,
I will experience exhilaration in
my enjoyment of life's
experiences.

October 13

As I think about my Savior,

it is
comforting to
know that I have been
blessed with an inexhaustible
supply of energy that is a reserve
upon which I may freely draw,
until my spirit has become
a "candle of the Lord."
(Proverbs 20:27).

If it is true
that we lose intrinsic
light as we succumb to worldly
cares, the judgment may be nothing
more than a measurement of the number of
foot-candles remaining that we bring to the Bar of
Justice. "Our birth" may after all, be only "a sleep and a
forgetting. The soul that rises with us, our life's star," has
perhaps "had elsewhere its setting, and cometh from afar.
Not in entire forgetfulness, and not in utter nakedness,
but trailing clouds of glory do we come from God."
In like manner do we return with honor,
to Him "Who is our Home."
(William Wordsworth).

October 14

As I think about my Savior,

I marvel that He
would send a message
of hope and reconciliation to
a world that has not only refused
to acknowledge His existence,
but that has also exhausted
itself in an animated
denial of the
truth.

During
a long night of
apostasy that must
have seemed endless,
the poetry of the Prince of
Peace largely fell on deaf ears
and stirred few souls. "Is it not a
shame," asked William Tyndall in
1528, "that we Christians come
so oft to church in vain, when
he of four score years old
knoweth no more than
he that was born
yesterday?"

October 15

As I think about my Savior,

my attention turns to the downtrodden, the friendless, the unappreciated, and those who feel that they are hopelessly mired in sin. I find that I am willing to bear the burdens of others, so "that they may be light, (and to) mourn with those that mourn; yea, and (to) comfort those that stand in need of comfort." (Mosiah 18:8-9).

As I throw open my arms to others, and give to them of my resources, I begin to recognize the truth in the declaration of the Savior, that "inasmuch as ye have done it unto the least of these, my brethren, ye have done it unto me." (Matthew 25:40).

October 16

As I think about my Savior,

I am
motivated to
undertake a program
of spiritual calisthenics to
stretch and tone up my
muscles as I continue
my journey back
to my celestial
home.

It
begins
in Bethlehem,
and then moves on to
Galilee and His ministry in
Judea; winds its way to Jerusalem,
Gethsemane, and Calvary, and finally
to an empty tomb outside the city walls.
During my own travels, I remain anxiously
engaged in good causes, and do many things
of my own free will and choice. I am an agent
unto myself, and independently bring to pass
much righteousness, realizing that His
power has always been within me.

October 17

As I think about my Savior,

and
about my
autobiographical
thread that leads all
the way back to heaven,
I am given hope to know
that I, "who am less than the
least of all saints" (Ephesians
3:8), was "in the beginning
with the Father."
(D&C 93:23).

I want
to make it my
ongoing mission to so
live that I qualify to regain
the glory of my former home. I
"have warmed both hands before the
fires of life. The rich spoils of memory
are mine. Mine, too, are the precious
experiences of today. However, the
best of life is hidden from my eyes
somewhere beyond the hills of
time." (William Mulock).

October 18

As I think about my Savior,

I will be
patient, and rather
than pushing my own
agenda, and pressing Him
for assistance that I do not
deserve and for which I
am unprepared, I will
wait for confirmation
that will come in
His own due
time.

Those who
demand outward
evidence of the power
of God as a condition for their
belief seek to circumvent the process
by which both faith and knowledge are
developed. As an adulterer, they seek
results but reject the related moral
element of responsibility. They
desire proof without having
first paid the price.

October 19

As I think about my Savior,

I can
see that in
spite of the fact
that the stream of His
gifts is uninhibited, it has
been rejected by a world that
is preoccupied with tangible
telestial treasures that are
really nothing more than
the terrain traps that
dot the uncertain
landscape
of life.

His gifts
include baptism,
a covenant of salvation,
the companionship of the Holy
Ghost, a covenant of justification,
the Sacrament, a covenant of
sanctification, and celestial
marriage, a covenant
of exaltation.

October 20

As I think about my Savior,

I see more
clearly how He has
individually custom
tailored the fabric of the
Gospel and stitched my
life experiences into
its pattern.

I cheerfully
display that tapestry
as a coat of many colors that
I may wear with confidence during
every season of my life. It contains not a
single shoddy stitch, and a thread pattern and
design that is spiritually coherent, that is tightly
woven to withstand every wind of adversity, and
that provides me with the elasticity I need in order
to initiate positive change. After my completion
of this transformative process, my spiritual
rebirth will have been one of generation,
and not only of maturation. I will be
satisfyingly surprised to learn
that I have become a new
creature in Christ.

October 21

As I think about my Savior,

it helps
if I put out of
my mind the relentless
stream of telestial trivia that
threatens to jam my channels of
communication with the Spirit, and
to knock my understanding of the
doctrines of the kingdom
out of alignment.

Leaving
those distractions
behind me allows me to
concentrate on the birth, ministry,
atonement, death, and resurrection of
Christ, that are all pertinent to the Great
Plan of eternal progression. The intangible
reward that I will certainly receive is to
"be perfected in the understanding of
(my) ministry, in theory, in principle,
and in doctrine, in all things
pertaining to the kingdom
of God on the earth."
(D&C 97:14).

October 22

As I think about my Savior,

the privileges and
promises of old, that were first
made to the fathers, are re-awakened in
my soul. As did Abraham, I will seek "for the
blessings of the fathers, and the right whereunto
I should be ordained to administer the same; having
been myself a follower of righteousness, desiring also
to be one who possessed great knowledge, and to be
a greater follower of righteousness, and to possess
a greater knowledge…to receive instructions,
and to keep the commandments of God."
(Abraham 1:2).

"The stars
fade away, the
sun himself grow
dim with age, and
nature sink in years.
But thou shalt flourish
in immortal youth, unhurt
amidst the war of elements,
the wreck of matter, and
the crash of worlds."
(Joseph Addison).

October 23

As I think about my Savior,

it is
the prayer of
my heart that He will
treat the Saints gently and
tenderly when He comes in "his
glory, and in his power, and in his
might, majesty, and dominion," and
tramples out the vintage where the
grapes of wrath have for so long
been stored, as the day of
judgment draws nigh.
(Alma 12:15).

"Sound the great trumpet
for our freedom. Raise the banner
for gathering our exiles from the four
corners of the earth into our own land."
(Jewish Prayer). The Gospel will be preached
to the elect of God, who will then rally around its
standard, ultimately to congregate with the Saints in
the stakes of Zion. Then, the work will commence
in earnest, "whereby his people may be gathered
home to the land of their inheritance. And I
will go before them, saith the Father."
(3 Nephi 21:28-29).

October 24

As I think about my Savior, and consecrate my efforts to His service, I more fully appreciate the blessings that are related to the portentous principle of sacrifice.

The Mortal Messiah urged those of us in bondage to go the second mile, and to double our stride. Thus, would be removed the veil of insensitivity to our destiny. When we are wrapped up in ourselves, we make very small packages. Selfishness and selflessness are mutually exclusive qualities. The former will destroy our ability to feel, while the latter will build character and our capacity to love.

October 25

As I think about my Savior,

I easily
find myself
caught up in the
experience, as I am
carried away on
the concentric
waves of the
Spirit.

When
you really feel
something, you can
express it. If you can't,
you do not feel it strongly
enough. "Once, in a sermon,
B.H. Roberts described Christ
and the raising of Lazarus from
the dead. So vivid were his images,
and so moving his presence, that the
audience was carried with him. When,
in a loud voice, he repeated the Master's
words: 'Lazarus, come forth!' the entire
congregation involuntarily jumped
to its feet." (Truman Madsen).

October 26

As I think about my Savior,

I
appreciate the
impressive obstetrical
skills with which He has
delivered me from death,
to enjoy a second birth
and liberation from
the intensive care
unit of life.

I
rejoice
that I have been
Born Again, to enjoy
a covenant consciousness
that sows confidence. I know
what He expects of me, and that
His blessings follow my obedience.
I have a testimony that His Church
is based on unchanging principles,
and that the requirements to gain
salvation will forever be the
same for all of His
children.

October 27

As I think about my Savior

and
hold firmly to
His revealed truth
with the eye of faith, I
know that the mysteries
of the kingdom will be
unfolded to my view
as well as to my
understanding,
so that I may
"see."

Joseph's description of
his revelatory experiences has
provided us with a word portrait
that is an illuminated manuscript into
his soul. He said: "We began to have the
scriptures laid open to our understandings,
and the true meaning and intention of their
more mysterious passages revealed unto
us in a manner which we never could
attain to previously, nor ever
before had thought of."
(J.S.H. 1:74).

October 28

As I think about my Savior,

I
realize
that even my
best efforts will
count for nothing,
unless I am "a vessel
unto honour, sanctified,
and meet for the master's
use, and prepared unto
every good work."
(2 Timothy 2:21).

In the
scriptures, works are
generally associated only with
obedience to the commandments. In this
sense, Paul taught that "not the hearers of the
law are just before God, but the doers of the law
shall be justified." (Romans 2:13). "Good works,"
Martin Luther explained, "do not make a good
man, but a good man does good works."
And what is it that makes us good?
It is simply faith in God,
and in Christ!

October 29

As I think about my Savior,

within my
heartstrings there is
generated the witness of
His power, and of "His breath
(that) kindleth coals, and a flame
(that) goeth out of his mouth." (Job
41:21). Thus, has the Lord's prophet
symbolically described the way that
I feel, as well. His words are as a
firebrand that ignites my soul
with the flame of faith.

"His word
was in mine heart as
a burning fire shut up in
my bones, and I was weary
with forbearing, and I could not
stay." (Jeremiah 20:9). Fire and smoke
remind us of the glory of celestial realms.
"God Almighty Himself dwells in eternal fire.
Flesh and blood cannot go there, for all corruption
is devoured by that fire." (Joseph Smith). Simply
put: "Our God is a consuming fire."
(Hebrews 12:29).

October 30

As I think about my Savior,

and I
give Him my
my undivided
attention, He is
revealed to
me anew.

Although it may be
summarily brushed off by a
world that has lost its appetite, there
lies before us a virtual smorgasbord of
religious experience waiting to be enjoyed by
those who have a discriminating spiritual palate.
Manger scenes may encourage me, hymns may be
inspiring, and gift giving may put me in the mood,
but if I want to receive His sure witness, I will find
it in dreams and visions, by voices, promptings, a
burning in my bosom, or in strokes of inspiration.
However it may be received, I stand with Parley
P. Pratt, who declared: "I have received the
holy anointing, and I can never rest until
the last enemy is conquered, death
destroyed, and truth reigns
triumphant."

October 31

As I think about my Savior,

His majesty,
power, and dominion
stand in sharp contrast to
the simplicity of the scene at
the manger, that rivets my
attention on the humble
circumstances that
surrounded His
birth.

As the Church
and the Kingdom of God
grow to encompass a world-
wide membership, we must not
forget the simplicity of the pattern
that makes up the Gospel tapestry.
We must beware, lest what we do
organizationally becomes nothing
more than embellishment. As we
build up individuals, we must
never confuse gratuitous
adornment for what is
really important.

"Ye are the light of the world."
(Matthew 5:14).

November 1

As I think about my Savior,

I try
to imagine the
poverty of the scene in
Bethlehem, and how
He was wrapped in
swaddling clothes,
and laid in a
manger.

Even as
we think about the
humble circumstances
that surrounded the Nativity,
we can be certain that as He grew to
manhood, Jesus of Nazareth enjoyed few
temporal advantages. Nevertheless, He was
abundantly blessed with remarkable gifts.
Scripture reveals that "he served under
his father, and he spake not as other
men, neither could he be taught;
for he needed not that any
man should teach him."
(J.S.T. Matthew 2:25).

November 2

As I think about my Savior,

but
at the same
time feel estranged
from the Spirit and far
from Him, I must concede
that it is not He, but I,
who has moved.

We
can be certain
that our Creator is
no respecter of persons.
He does not draw up sides,
or pick and choose which of His
children He will favor, and which He
will neglect or ignore. He respects the Plan
of Salvation and honors its guiding principle
that has been described as the Prime Directive.
His impartiality is eminently fair, and He will not
unnecessarily interfere in our affairs. We are all
"the children of (our) Father who is in heaven,
(Who) maketh his sun to rise on the
evil, (as well as) on the good."
(3 Nephi 12:45).

November 3

As I think about my Savior

and feel
the bite of the crisp
autumn air, I can sense
the reassuring radiance of
"love's pure light" at the
break of "the dawn of
redeeming grace."
(Franz Gruber).

Without the
protection afforded by
that light, I risk being seduced
by a siren song that creates an insatiable
desire for telestial trinkets. When my vision is
blurred, I may confuse life on the strait and narrow
path with a vacation in Idumea. Then I will lose power,
purpose, and focus. If I have grown to depend more on
my own strength than upon my spiritual preparedness,
I will be more inclined in times of crisis to grasp at the
world's goods, rather than to drop to my knees, hold
tightly to my faith, seek out the tender mercies
of my Father in Heaven, and with His help,
work my way through my challenges
all the way back into His Rest.

November 4

As I think about my Savior,

and pause to listen, I
can hear with my heart the
urgency in His voice, as He
begs me to come out of the
cold and from the cares
of the world, into the
warmth of His
embrace.

All
those who
have accepted His
sweet solicitation have
discovered for themselves how
association with the Saints and the
institution of His Church can become
"their refuge from confusion and religious
doubts, their instructor in principle, doctrine,
and righteousness, as well as their guide in
matters of faith and morals. They have a
conjoint ownership in it with Jesus
Christ, which…is recognized in
the latter part of the title."
(B.H. Roberts).

November 5

As I think about my Savior,

my
vitals and
bowels will be
healthy and strong,
and properly perform
their functions, but more
importantly, my spiritual
hunger will be satisfied
as my heart embraces
true and virtuous
principles.

I hope to be as
focused as a cat on the
prowl as I "press forward
with a steadfastness in Christ."
I hope that I may exhibit a child-
like faith. (2 Nephi 31:20). I hope
that I will be able to declare: "I'll
lay all my fortunes at your feet
and follow you, my lord,
all over the world."
(Shakespeare).

November 6

As I think about my Savior,

and I
consent in my heart
to the law of God, I expect
it to be as a rushing of many
waters that ushers in the perfect
law of liberty. I expect to enjoy
the therapeutic feeling that
abundantly prepares me
to face the future.
(See James 1:25).

Those
who yield their
will to higher powers, and
allow themselves to be molded
in the image and likeness of their
Master, are "meek, patient, courteous,
and merciful to their neighbours." They
have been "altered and fashioned like
unto Christ. Why then should they
doubt but that God hath forgiven
them, and chosen them, and
put his spirit in them?"
(William Tyndale).

November 7

As I think about my Savior,

I
understand
that, ultimately,
He lived and died
for one reason only:
So that we might live
as an extended family
in the eternities, where
we will finally begin to
exercise our abilities
as the children
of God.

Wherever
my journeys may
take me, I am comforted
by the gentle promise that
as I engage the Church, I will
never be a stranger and will never
feel like a foreigner, but instead will
be a fellow citizen with the Saints,
as I take up residence in "the
household of God."
(Ephesians 2:19).

November 8

As I think about my Savior,

it
warms
the cockles
of my heart to
know that, all over
the world, the old and
hallowed story is still
being repeated with
wondering awe, to
His children of
all ages.

The
Greatest Story Ever
Told is most convincingly
passed on by the authorized and
inspired servants of the Lord, called to
preach the first principles and ordinances
of His Gospel to every nation, kindred, tongue,
and people. Faith will increase in the world
"by hearing those who are sent from God
and preacheth His promises."
(William Tyndale).

November 9

As I think about my Savior

through the
clarifying medium of
faith, I am transported to
the Holy Land, where I can
see with my own eyes the
Star of Bethlehem, as it
twinkles brightly with
hope, high in the sky
above a humble
manger.

Belief is a
mental assent to
the truth or actuality
of something, without the
moral element of responsibility
that we call faith. The process by which
faith is developed is one of testing. The Lord
gives certain principles, and by our obedience,
blessings and power follow. Confirmation of
the reality comes only after we act in faith.
It is in this sense, that "faith, if it hath
not works, is dead, being alone."
(James 2:17).

November 10

As I think about my Savior,

I realize that His love can bridge the gap
between the world of everyday and
a promised land that lies just
over the horizon.

Every
one of us may
experience a little bit
of heaven on earth if we
accept the invitation to come
unto Christ. That world to which
we have all been invited is a realm of
spirit, of sensory fragrance and delight,
sound, substance, and color. It is the realm
of human associations, gratitude, loyalty, and
appreciation, and of selflessness, helpfulness,
and of forgiveness, and of friendship, love,
and compassion. It is the realm of growth
and transcendence, of truth discovered
and accepted, of beauty created and
enjoyed, of goodness deepened
and made manifest in life.
(See P.A. Christensen, "A
Land Unpromised and
Unearned").

November 11

As I think about my Savior,

I am
blessed to
experience a
witness equal in
power to that which
was extended to the
humble shepherds
in the fields near
Bethlehem.

They
were the first
to hear the heavenly
choir and see the angels,
and the lesson they have left
us is that the poor, the unlearned,
the common person, and the native
born, may come unto Christ. In many
passages, the scriptures teach of the
universality of God's concern for
His children, all of whom may
experience for themselves
the love of their Lord
and Savior.

November 12

As I think about my Savior,

I
want
to share my
testimony with the
world that our Father
has glorified and exalted
Him, and has "given Him
a name which is above
every (other) name"
under the heavens.
(Philippians 2:9).

"Unto us
a Child is born,
unto us a Son is given;
and the government shall be
upon His shoulder: and His name
shall be called Wonderful, Counsellor,
the Mighty God, the Everlasting Father,
the Prince of Peace." (Isaiah 9:6). The Savior
earned every one of these titles "because
of the glory His Father had given
Him before He was born."
(Joseph Smith).

November 13

As I think about my Savior,

I
raise my
eyes to look
past the limited
horizon of my sight,
so that I might, "with a
vision splendid, be on my
way attended" by both
signs and wonders
in the heavens.
(Longfellow).

I join
the wise men
of old, as they ask:
"Where is he that is born
King of the Jews? For we
have seen his star in the East
and are come to worship him."
(Matthew 2:2). With awakening
awe, it strikes me that, as a celestial
supernova, the Light of the World has
endured for 2,000 years, and even now
invites me to follow a stellar example.

November 14

As I think about my Savior,

I will
always try
to remember
that the Kingdom of
God is more than just
the exchange of gifts
at Christmas time,
and a delicious
dinner with
family.

The eternities are not
focused, as I sometimes seem to be,
on a scramble for scarce resources. Even
now, there is enough, and to spare. The Lord has
promised that the fulness of the earth can be mine.
"Yea, all things which come of the earth, in the
season thereof, are made for the benefit and
the use of man, both to please the eye and
to gladden the heart; Yea, for food and
for raiment, for taste and for smell,
to strengthen the body and
to enliven the soul."
(D&C 59:15-19).

November 15

As I think about my Savior,

regardless of my
temporal circumstances, I
count myself fortunate to have
become "exceedingly rich, because
of (my) prosperity in Christ."
(4 Nephi 1:23).

We
remember
the Wise Men,
who had the proper
credentials as well as the
requisite frills to enter the
royal palace of haughty King
Herod, and boldly ask: "Where
is he that is born King of the Jews?
For we have seen his star in the east,
and are come to worship him." (Matthew
2:1-2). Their gift was the lesson that the
learned, the notable, and the foreign
born may come unto Christ, and
that telestial trinkets pale in
comparison to the gifts
of testimony and of
saving faith.

November 16

As I think about my Savior,

I ponder the poverty of the scene at the manger, even as I realize that I am "less than the dust of the earth."
(Helaman 12:7).

Benjamin was addressing me when he related our "nothingness" to our debt to God. As one speaking low, out of the dust, He has taught me that if I would praise Him, and serve Him with my whole soul, yet would I be an unprofitable servant. (See Mosiah 2:20-21). This is because my debt to Him is completely beyond my ability to pay, and there is nothing that I can do to oblige Him to me. But He does not ask me to settle my account with Him; He only requires that I keep His commandments to the best of my ability and to repent when I do not. The rest is left up to Him. Ultimately, it is by His grace alone that I enjoy salvation.

November 17

As I think about my Savior

with a
confidence that is
unshakable, my conviction
is bolstered, my faith replaces
my fear, and I receive a quiet
reassurance that "today is
a good day to die."
(Crazy Horse).

"Then out
spake brave Horatius,
the Captain of the Gate: To
every man upon this earth, death
cometh soon or late. And how can man
die better than facing fearful odds, for the
ashes of his fathers, and the temples of his gods?"
("Horatius," Thomas Macaulay). For those who have
unshakable testimonies of the Gospel, today and every
day is a good day to die. They fight a good fight, and if
they have not yet finished their course, they at least can
clearly see the finish line ahead. They keep the faith.
(Tasunka Witko, known as Crazy Horse, was a
powerful holy man of the Oglala Sioux, who
rode into battle unafraid of the bullets
that whizzed past his horse).

November 18

As I think about my Savior,

I travel
across the years
to the Holy Land,
where I respond to the
call "Adeste Fidelis,"
or "O come let us
adore Him."
(John Wade).

In my
mind's eye, I
go there to worship
"on bended knee, Christ the
Lord, the newborn King." ("Angels
We Have Heard on High"). "Outwardly,
God disguised him not, but made him like
other men, and sent him into the world to
offer himself for us a sacrifice of a sweet
savour, to kill the stench of our sins,
that God himself should smell
them no more, nor think
on them any more."
(William Tyndale).

November 19

As I think about my Savior,

I give Him
the credit for my
successes, lest I
be caught up
in the snare
of conceit.

How
rapidly
are we "lifted
up in pride; yea,
how quick to boast."
(Helaman 12:5). And yet,
how great an example were
the wise men of the East. They
may have been Zoroastrian Magi,
wearing the trappings of wealth and
position, and bearing costly gifts, but it
was their humility that compelled them
to make the arduous journey from the
East, to Bethlehem. It is significant
that over 2,000 years later, we
still refer to them as
"wise men."

November 20

As I think about my Savior,

I
hope that my
thanksgiving will
have less to do with
turkey, and more to do
with a gratitude that
will be sustainable
throughout the
year.

What
am I to do,
if I have only
recently cultivated
the trait of gratitude?
"Don't be discouraged if
you haven't been especially
grateful," encouraged Joseph
Wirthlin. "Rejoice and think of
what an impression you will
make on those who thought
they knew you! Think of
how surprised they
will be!"

November 21

As I think about my Savior,

I am
able to put my
skyrocketing credit
card balance in proper
perspective as I realize
how it has been easily
eclipsed by my even
greater debt to
Him.

"Each of us
lives on a kind of
spiritual credit. One day
the account will be closed, and
a settlement demanded. However
casually we may view it now, when that
day comes and foreclosure is imminent, we
will look about in restless agony for someone,
anyone, to help us. And by eternal law, mercy
cannot be extended save there be one who is
both willing and able to assume our debt,
and pay the price, and arrange the
terms of our redemption."
(Boyd K. Packer).

November 22

As I think about my Savior,

I remember that it was
with wondering awe that the
Wise Men saw the star in heaven
and were encouraged to press
on toward Bethlehem.

As
the Magi
plodded through
desert wastes during
their long journey, they
were guided by a new star
that appeared over Bethlehem,
so that the mighty and high-born
might also stand as witnesses of the
heavenly choir and the babe Who lay
in the manger. But they took no honor
unto themselves, and after leaving their
gifts of gold, frankincense, and myrrh,
they discreetly left Judea by another
way. Just as Isaiah had foreseen, so
had it come to pass: Those who
had walked in darkness had
"seen a great light."
(Isaiah 9:2).

November 23

As I think about my Savior,

I hear all the bells of Christendom ring out the message of salvation.

The
disciples of the
Lord publish peace, in
contrast to the contention that is
Babylon's effluent discharge. The
Saints are transformed from the inside,
but Babylon's rough exterior repels reform,
which if it comes at all, is from the outside. His
people act, while Babylon is manipulated. The Lord's
disciples embrace self-determination; Babylon mistakes
license for freedom. His people understand and correctly
exercise moral agency. Babylon substitutes government
paternalism for free will. Disciples honor the celestial
principle of consecration. Babylon worships socialism
as its salvation, and engages in gluttony, conspicuous
consumption, and making merry, with the certain
expectation that tomorrow she will die, and
so she will. The children of the Lord
prepare for the worst but hope
for the best, for peace on
earth and good will
toward men.

November 24

As I think about my Savior,

I find myself in
a place of quiet solitude
where I can gaze up into
heaven to the very same
stars that looked down
upon the scene in
Bethlehem over
2,000 years
ago.

It was
Jesus Christ our
Redeemer, Who asked
Job: "Where wast thou when
I laid the foundations of the earth?
When the morning stars sang together, and
all the sons of God shouted for joy? (Job 38:4 & 7).
So there would be no mistake about it, the Lord has
affirmed: "I was in the beginning with the Father, and
am the Firstborn. Ye were also in the beginning with
the Father." (D&C 93:21 & 23). We have all come
from His throne trailing clouds of glory, as
did those morning "stars of heaven."
(Revelation 12:4).

November 25

As I think about my Savior,

the
story of His
birth is just the
catalyst I need to
propel me to the
discovery of the
personal levels
of experience
with divine
realities.

It isn't enough to
know about His birth
by reading the account in
Luke, or by listening to others
speak of Him. I must know Him
through bonds of common experience
and shared feeling. My religious conviction
must be involved not only with discovery, but
also with recovery. My destiny is not just union,
but also reunion, with divine realities, and my
religious recognition is my re-acquaintance
with what I have already known. It is my
re-awakening to eternal possibilities.

November 26

As I think about my Savior,

I recall the sound
of hopeful anticipation
provided by Salvation Army
bells, and I am prompted
to extend my charity to
those who are less
fortunate than I.

In the
meantime, distracted
shoppers rush by without
noticing, on their way to spending
$5.00 on a Starbuck's Cinnamon Dolce
Latte Venti, or $2.50 on a bottle of designer
water at the supermarket. People of affluence
too often "beat my people to pieces, and grind the
faces of the poor, saith the Lord of Hosts." (2 Nephi
13:15). And yet, there is hope that when we hear the
bells peal "more loud and deep," they will reveal
that "God is not dead, nor doth he sleep. The
wrong shall fail, the right prevail, with
peace on earth" and "good will to
men" throughout the year.
(Longfellow).

November 27

As I think about my Savior

and I greet
the changing of the
seasons, I have already
anticipated the holidays, when
I will hang my stocking on the
mantle with care, hoping
that Santa will fill it
with all sorts of
treats.

I should
know better, for it
is God, and not Saint
Nick, Who knows exactly
what nourishment is best for
me, at what frequency, quantity,
and in what proportion. I must not
question His good judgment. At the
same time, I hope that I may also
remember that "I can never get
enough of what I don't need,
because what I don't need
won't satisfy me."
(Dallin Oaks).

November 28

As I think about my Savior,

I look forward to a
wonderful family dinner,
complete with a turkey with
mashed potatoes and gravy,
or a goose with all the
trimmings.

Even as I delight in a cornucopia of
nourishing food, the recesses of my mind
are stimulated by the haunting refrain: "Don't
let it be forgot, that once there was a spot for one
brief shining moment, that was known as Camelot."
(Jay Lerner). So I resist the gustatory distractions of the
season, and renew my efforts to press forward, feasting
instead upon the word of Christ. If "this is my quest,
to follow that star, no matter how hopeless, no
matter how far, to fight for the right, without
question or pause, to be willing to march
into hell for a heavenly cause," I know
that "my heart will lie peaceful and
calm when I'm laid to my rest."
and I will leave the world
itself a better place.
(Joe Darion).

November 29

As I think about my Savior,

I expect that my concentration will be assaulted by headlines that shout out the encouraging news that consumers, still recovering from Thanksgiving feasts, have spent billions of dollars in a single frenzied Friday of gratuitous shopping excess.

Items "on sale" all across the land will encourage me to max out my credit card limit so that I can save money. Retailers pray for a lucrative Chritma $eason. Have we all gone mad? A judge asked the jury: "Have you reached a verdict?" "We have, your Honor," responded the foreman. "We find the defendant not guilty by reason of insanity." To which news the Judge exclaimed, "What? All twelve of you?" We all seem to go collectively crazy toward the end of the year, as we feverishly attempt to outspend each other in futile efforts to demonstrate our generosity.

November 30

As I think about my Savior,

I
find myself
trying not to shout,
cry, or pout, because
I've heard that "Santa
Claus is comin' to town."
(Fred Coots & Haven Gillespie).

Spoiler
alert! It is the Lord
Jesus Christ, and not Santa
Claus, Who will soon arrive to
establish a thousand years of peace
on the earth. He knows us better than
anyone else. He knows when we've been
sleeping, and He knows when we're awake.
He knows when we've been bad or good, so
we need to be good for goodness' sake. There
is no one else who knows our thoughts and
the intent of our hearts. "O how great the
holiness of our God!" cried Jacob. "For
he knoweth all things, and there is
not anything save he knows it."
(2 Nephi 9:20).

> This is to my Father's glory, that you
> bear much fruit, and clarify your-
> selves with Heaven.
> (Matthew 3:16)

"Let your light so shine before men, that they may see your good works, and glorify your Father which is in heaven."
(Matthew 5:16).

December 1

As I think about my Savior

around
Christmastime,
whimsical visions
of fairies, sugar plums,
and other holiday delights
dance in my head, clamoring
for underserved attention.

"Every
one that thirsteth,
come ye to the waters, and
he that hath no money; come ye,
buy, and eat; yea, come, buy wine and
milk without money and without price." Thus,
has the prophet Isaiah exhorted me: "Wherefore
do ye spend money for that which is not bread?
And you labour for that which satisfieth not?
Hearken diligently unto me, and eat ye that
which is good, and let your soul delight
itself in fatness." (Isaiah 55:1-3). We
seem to have a free pass to load
on the calories of contrition
that inexorably lead to
our just desserts.

December 2

As I think about my Savior,

I am
drawn to
the lamp that
was first ignited
in heaven with one
purpose in mind: To
give light to both
my days and my
nights.

"And
behold, there
shall a new star arise,
such an one as ye never
have beheld; and this also shall
be a sign unto you." (Helaman 14:5).
Even the Zoroastrian priests from the East
saw the light, and perceived its significance.
Arriving in Jerusalem after the Savior's birth,
they inquired of King Herod: "Where is he
that is born King of the Jews? For we
have seen his star in the east, and
are come to worship him."
(Matthew 2:2).

December 3

As I think about my Savior,

I
will not
be distracted
by Frosty, who,
along with Rudolph
and the other reindeer,
always seems to be in a
competition with the
Nativity for yard
space.

It is very difficult to keep Jesus
the focus of our thoughts at Christmas,
even as we journey with Him along the road
that is less traveled. But it is that path alone that
climbs steadily to the pinnacle of our worship.
Awaiting discovery there is a celestial beacon
whose sweeping light shines above the cares
and extends beyond the comprehension of
the world. It stands as a sentinel over a
city in the clouds where both angels
and cherubim join mere mortals
to cry Hosanna to His
holy name.

December 4

As I think about my Savior,

I ponder the spectacle
of the morning stars who
gathered together to create
a spontaneous and rapturous
flash mob at the Holy Birth.

The
Lord Jesus
Christ is the physical
expression of the Rock of
Revelation (Matthew 16:18)
and the personification of the
"One Eternal God." (Alma 11:44).
We accept His word as "the doctrine
of Christ, and the only and true doctrine
of the Father, and of the Son, and of the Holy
Ghost, which is one God, without end." (3 Nephi
18:12). It is my testimony that the morning stars and
all the sons of God were mustered out of heaven
itself to come to earth, so that they might shout
for joy as they bore their fervent testimony to
shepherds who were quietly tending their
flocks by night in the fields outside
the little town of Bethlehem.
(See Job 38:7 & Luke 2:9).

December 5

As I think about my Savior,

the symbols of the season, with gaily decorated ornaments hanging on the tree, remind me of the rights that properly belong to the priesthood.

These
are crude
imitations of
the orb of authority
that is described in the
scriptures as a "Liahona."
(See 1 Nephi 16:10). That ball
or director is "inseparably connected
to the powers of heaven, and the powers
of heaven cannot be controlled nor handled
only upon the principles of righteousness."
(D&C 121:36). This definitive declaration
emphasizes that the Church is driven by
the power of a priesthood that traces
its authority directly to "the author
of eternal salvation unto all
them that obey him."
(Hebrews 5:9).

December 6

As I think about my Savior,

I
realize
that at one
magical moment
upon a midnight
clear, the world
was instantly
changed for
the better.

In
every clime,
and in nations far
and wide, the Gospel of
Jesus Christ has spread to
those who hear the message of
salvation in their native language.
For "it is as good to preach to swine
as to men if it be preached in a tongue
they understand not. How can I believe
the truth and promises which God hath
sworn, while thou tellest them to me in
a tongue which I understand not."
(William Tyndale).

December 7

As I think about my Savior,

I am moved to acknowledge the innocence of the child that lies within each of us.

"One of the greatest tragedies in life is not children who are afraid of the dark, but men who are afraid of the light." (Plato). What a heartbreak it is to see what dies in us while we are yet alive. It is by the grace of God that our eyes are opened and we sacrifice ourselves through His love to create a little bit of heaven on earth, as we provide assistance to others who are making the journey to Christ.

December 8

As I think about my Savior,

at
one and
the same time,
I visualize Him as
a Babe in swaddling
clothes, as the mortal
Messiah, and as a
glorified God
in heaven.

Without a
relationship with the
Savior, what could have
been our pivotal experiences of
mortality must be neutralized, and
ultimately, they will count for nothing.
For "this is life eternal, that they might know
thee the only true God, and Jesus Christ whom
thou hast sent." (John 17:3). Joseph Smith declared
that "there are but a very few beings in the world
who understand rightly the nature of God." If
we cannot understand His character, how
can we possibly be expected to
comprehend ourselves?

December 9

As I think about my Savior,

and look up into the crisp
air of a winter sky, I can imagine
the thrill of those whose eyes were
dazzled when "a new star did
appear" in the heavens.
(3 Nephi 1:21).

With that
bright beacon of
hope twinkling overhead
in the night sky, the Church
of Jesus Christ in the New World
became a third class of witnesses to
the birth of the Savior, joining the Wise
Men and the shepherds in the fields. As a
result, His people in Zarahemla began "to have
peace in the land. And there were no contentions."
(3 Nephi 1:23-24). The star in the East was symbolic
of their focus on the Savior. His Gospel was their
fortification, obedience to the covenants was their
sanctuary, and reliance upon the light was their
protection against the prince of darkness,
whose murky influence would very
soon be sweeping across
the land.

December 10

As I think about my Savior,

the shepherds of old remind me that
the poor, the unlearned, the common
person, and the native born, may
come unto Him just as easily
as those of a lofty station or
with powerful influence.

The
Apostle
Paul assured the
Corinthian Saints that
if they remained steadfast, in
no matter what circumstances they
might find themselves, no matter what
cards they might have been dealt in life, in no
matter what cruel twist of fate they might think
themselves trapped, ultimately, all things would be
theirs, for they were "Christ's, and Christ is God's."
(1 Corinthians 3:23). My hope of salvation and a
glorious resurrection hinges upon this truth,
however dimly I may now perceive it, or
how hesitantly I may now believe it,
or how timidly I may now act
upon my promptings.

December 11

As I think about my Savior,

I contrast
the frenzy of the
madding crowds at the
shopping malls with the
reflection of introspection
enjoyed by the faithful
who gather in their
quiet places of
worship.

As
soon as
I am moved to
plumb the depths of
my spiritual core, I will be
compelled to cry out: "Blessed
be the name of He that cometh in
the name of the Lord; thou art my God,
and I will bless thee; thou art my God, I will
exalt thee." (Psalms 118:28). My celebration
of His miraculous birth and His holy
mission will expand exponentially
to encompass the whole of
my existence.

December 12

As I think about my Savior,

I can visualize
Santa's elves, who, as
symbols of the season, sit at
their workbenches at the North Pole,
tirelessly working in my behalf to
create special gifts made
with me in mind.

I am, and
forever will be, God's
junior partner, and never
His equal, but I do know what
it feels like to be in business with
Him. When I work hard, and the sweat
drips off the end of my nose, I realize that it
is my Father in Heaven Who has given me the
capacity to work, and I am thankful to Him for
whatever talent and energy I may have. When I
survey the fruits of my labor, I try to envision the
greater purpose for which my rich blessings have
come. I hope to be a good steward, and if by His
grace my talents are multiplied, my enjoyment
and satisfaction will reach their zenith when
they are put to use for the benefit of others.

December 13

As I think about my Savior,

I
can see
why it was
not with the high
and the mighty, but
with the poor, and the
mean, and the lowly,
that our Savior
lived on
earth.

Perhaps it was the humble
circumstances surrounding His
birth, or His unpretentious lifestyle, that
explains His intolerance of the Pharisees, who
were obsessed with public demonstrations of blind
obedience to outward ordinances and observances.
He characterized them as whited sepulchres, full
of dead men's bones. In other words, they were
hypocrites, and their actions were a façade,
for they only pretended to be pious,
when they were, in reality, just
going through the motions.

December 14

As I think about my Savior,

the Spirit quietly
reminds me that He
knows when I am
sleeping, and
He knows
when I'm
awake.

He
knows
when I've been
bad or good, so I must
be good for goodness' sake!
Whether or not paper and ink,
or even tablets of metal or stone,
survive the ravages of time, God
will be able to read the record of
my life, for it is engraven in my
sinews. He Who created me
can read the tapestry that
is stitched into my soul
as easily as He could
any printed
text.

December 15

As I think about my Savior,

I am
warmed
by the fire of
the friendships
that I share with
others.

The
celebration
of His birth is a
joyous time when
salutations of "Merry
Christmas" and "Happy
Holidays" come from our
hearts as well as from our lips,
and our eggnog toasts reflect our
true yearnings and our hope that
the Lord will bless and keep us;
that His countenance may shine
upon us, and bring us peace;
that our hearts may be full,
our lives long, and our
days as sweet as an
Irish song.

December 16

As I think about my Savior,

and the Magi's gifts of gold, frankincense, and myrrh, I recognize that these are but shadows of the greatest gift of all, Who was Christ the Lord.

I can be
sure that I will
receive His grace
proportionately as I
conform to the standard
of personal righteousness
that is key to the Gospel Plan.
Thus, I have been commanded to
"grow in grace" (D&C 50:40) until I
am sanctified and justified "thru the
grace of our Lord and Savior Jesus
Christ." (D&C 20:30-32). It is in
this sense that Nephi declared
that we are saved by grace
only "after all we can do,"
which is primarily to
repent of our sins.
(2 Nephi 25:23).

December 17

As I think about my Savior,

and in
particular, as I
consider Mary's love
for her newborn Son, I
realize how important it is
that babies be delivered into the
protective care of mothers who are
not only good at changing diapers, but
who, with a nurturing influence that
only they can provide, are good
at changing the world.

"And
she brought forth
her first-born son, and
wrapped him in swaddling
clothes, and laid him in a manger:
because there was no room for them
in the inn. ...And the child grew,
and waxed strong in spirit,
filled with wisdom; and
the grace of God was
upon him."
(Luke 2:40).

December 18

As I think about my Savior,

I
wonder
why it is that we
subject our little ones
to long lines at the
mall, just for the
chance to sit
on Santa's
lap.

I have
read in The Book
of Mormon about how
Jesus ministered so sweetly
and so tenderly to the Nephite
children; how He took them "one
by one, and blessed them, and prayed
unto the Father for them. ...And they
saw the heavens open, and they saw
angels descending out of heaven...
and they were encircled about
with fire; and the angels did
minister unto them."
(3 Nephi 17:21-24).

December 19

As I think about my Savior

at
this
time of
year, I can
be sure that
someone on a
sidewalk will be
ringing a bell, to
help me keep
Him in my
heart.

As I think
about the season
of the Savior's birth, I
remember the motion picture
classic of the silver screen, "It's a
Wonderful Life," and I try to envision
Clarence, the amiable angel who finally
earned his wings by saving George Bailey.
My heart is warmed, as I recall that it
was the tinkling of bells on the
Bailey's Christmas tree that
signaled his passage.

December 20

As I think about my Savior,

I am
grateful that God
so loved the world
that He created
mistletoe.

Most
character
traits need the
softening influence of
love before they can hope
to become celestial qualities.
Love is an aether that permits me
to catch a glimpse of heaven. It allows
me to bridge the gulf between the world of
everyday, and a holy land that is untinctured
and untresspassed. God dwells there, in Camelot,
and is the personification of the love that governs
His kingdom. He has provided us with the
mistletoe that grows profusely in His
realm, to be used as a back-up in
those special situations when
nothing else seems to
to be working.

December 21

As I think about my Savior

while
putting cookies and
milk on the mantle in my
anticipation of a visit from
Old Saint Nick, I need to
remember from Whom
it is that my real
gifts have
come.

At first light, early
on Christmas morning,
as I shake out the contents of
the stocking that has been hung by
the mantle with care, a cornucopia of
treats cascades onto the floor. Almost
immediately, it strikes me that Father
in Heaven has promised even greater
gifts beyond my wildest dreams. He
will throw open "the windows of
heaven, and pour out a blessing
that there shall not be room
enough to receive it."
(2 Nephi 24:10).

December 22

As I think about my Savior,

I am struck by the relentless
passage of time, as days that
have grown shorter and
shorter finally reach
a turning point.

In the waning days
of December, as yet another
year draws to a close, the winter
solstice reminds me that each dawn brings
me the gift of time, and heralds the hope and
promise of a brighter day. Perhaps my commission
should be to pay attention not only to the thought with
which I spend my time, but also to the diligence with which
I make time, to the care with which I find time, and also
to the discipline with which I take time. This creative
process provides more time for accomplishment in
my busy life. Perhaps this is why it is that an idle
mind is the devil's workshop. If I waste time,
or kill time, or even when I bide my time, I
damage my eternal self, for in an hour
when I think not "the harvest is past,
the summer is ended, and my
soul is not saved."
(D&C 56:16).

December 23

As I think about my Savior,

I become
empowered to look
across the years upon
the scene at the manger
in Bethlehem, and to be
amazed anew by the
miracle of His
birth.

"Come,
follow me," said
the Son of God, who then
extended the mind-expanding
challenge to be perfect, even as He
and His Father are perfect. Thus, did
the Lord reveal that the purpose of earth
life is to progress until we reflect both the
image and likeness of God. (Genesis 1:26).
We were born to mature as the offspring
of Heavenly Father. It is our destiny to
one day reflect His striking image or
countenance, that our visage might
reveal the likeness of His
divine nature.

December 24

As I think about my Savior,

I can
almost hear the
irritation in the voice
of the innkeeper who
impatiently barked
out that there
was no room
for them
at the
inn.

We
contrast his
impatient behavior
with the recurring teaching
moments that surely took place in
the home of Joseph and Mary, where
charity must have been practiced as well
as preached. I remember the observation of
Mother Teresa: "Kind words can be short
and easy to speak, but their echoes are
truly endless." I am sure that the
Holy Family personified that
wise observation.

December 25

As I think about my Savior,

it strikes
me that the proud
new Father was willing
to wait for 30 long years
before finally proclaiming
to the world: "This is my
beloved son, in whom
I am well pleased."
(Matthew 3:17).

The
ministry that
He commenced
will transform me
and gently lift me to
higher ground, to the
point where I might be
transfigured as He was.
In that day, my face will
shine as the sun, and my
raiment will radiate with
dazzling light that has
been nurtured by a
celestial fire.

December 26

As I think about my Savior,

the Spirit
transports me
to the scene at the
manger, where I am
amazed anew by
the miracle of
His birth.

"Come,
follow me,"
said the Son of God,
who extended the mind
expanding and all-encompassing
commission to be perfect, as He and
His Father in Heaven are perfect. Thus,
did the Lord reveal that the purpose of life
on earth is to progress until we have achieved
immortality and eternal life, when we will
have developed both the image and the
likeness of our Heavenly Father. We
will be able to give Him the greater
glory by reflecting not only His
striking features, but also
His noble character.

December 27

As I think about my Savior,

I
know that
His are the gifts
that keep on giving,
and that it is because of
Him alone that I have been
provided with my own
personal Christmas
miracle of sweet
forgiveness.

Is it
really too
much for Him
to ask that I forgive
others? Without my real
forgiveness of those who have
supposedly wronged me, the Plan
of Redemption breaks down for both
of us. Brigham Young declared: "He who
takes offense when none was intended
is a fool, and he who takes offense
when one was intended is
usually a fool."

December 28

As I think about my Savior,

and
the bonuses
often received
from employers
during the holidays,
I am reminded of the
performance-related gifts
that we, on the other hand,
so willingly give to Him.

It can be
embarrassing to admit
how often I vigorously protest,
even as I am pushed, pulled, pinched,
provoked, prodded, propelled, poked, and
pampered to proceed along the path that leads
to a blessing. "If our souls had rings, as do trees,
to measure the years of greatest personal growth,
the wide rings would likely reflect the years of
greatest moisture, but from tears, not rainfall.
The highest source of suffering appears to
be reserved for (those) who undergo
divine tutorial training."
(Neal Maxwell).

December 29

As I think about my Savior

while pawing
my way through the
technological trinkets that
are scattered about beneath
the tree, if nothing happens
when I flip the "on" switch,
I must conclude that
batteries are not
included.

Just
as soon as I have
determined to commence an
environmentally friendly search for an
inexhaustible supply of celestial energy to
stimulate me to follow my star, I need look no
further than to a Holy Child lying upon a bed of
straw in Bethlehem. The Savior may have been
thinking of His own birth, when He revealed
to Joseph Smith: "Verily, I say unto you,
that as many as receive me, to them
will I give power to become
the sons of God."
(D&C 11:30).

December 30

As I think about my Savior,

I
may
decide to
leave in place
for a while longer,
the festive décor that
gently reminds me
that He is, after
all, the reason
we celebrate
Christmas.

When
virtue garnishes
my thoughts without
ceasing, then my confidence
will wax strong, and the doctrine
of the priesthood will distil upon my
head as the dews from heaven. When
my heart is thus full of the love of God,
the Holy Ghost will comfortably settle
in as my constant companion.
(See D&C 121:45).

December 31

As I think about my Savior,

I recall with
melancholy that
"the year is dying in
the night." I must take
courage, and prepare
for the morrow, to
"ring in the new."
(Tennyson).

The Savior
knew that I would
live in a world where the
distinctions between good and
evil would be blurred. Spiritual Babylon
is all around me, and so I need to be vigilant
because "vice is a monster of so frightful mien, as
to be hated needs but to be seen; Yet seen too oft,
familiar with her face, we first pity, then endure,
then embrace." (Alexander Pope). If I am to
recognize virtue and cleave unto every
good thing, I must resolve to do it
not only as the year is dying in
the night, but also as I ring
in the new.

"Be ye therefore perfect, even as your Father which is in heaven is perfect."
(Matthew 5:48).

About the Author

Phil Hudson and his wife Jan, have been married nearly 50 years, and have 7 children and over 20 grandchildren. They enjoy whiling away summer days with their family at their cabin, on the shores of Priest Lake, the crown jewel of North Idaho. Phil had a successful family dental practice in Spokane, Washington for 43 years, before retiring in 2015. In his free time, if he and Jan are not visiting their loved ones, he can be found roaming through Pacific Northwest woods, boating on the lake, cycling up mountain passes, riding his motorcycle along forest trails, or snowbiking in winters' deep powder along the Selkirk Crest. He always seems to find the time to write down his thoughts on his laptop, but appreciates Isaac Asimov's frustration when he was asked: "If you knew that you only had 10 minutes left to live, what would you do?" Without hesitation, Asimov answered: "I'd type faster."

"Suffer the little children to come unto me,
and forbid them not: for of such
is the kingdom of God."
(Mark 10:14)

Also by the Author

Essays: Spray From The Ocean Of Thought
Essays: Ripples On A Pond
Essays: Serendipitous Meanderings
Essays: Presents Of Mind
Essays: Mental Floss
Essays: Fitness Training For The Mind And Spirit

Book of Mormon Commentary: Born In The Wilderness
Book of Mormon Commentary: Voices From The Dust
Book of Mormon Commentary: Journey To Cumorah

Minute Musings: Volume One
Minute Musings: Volume Two
Minute Musings: Volume Three

Discovering William Tyndale

Diode Laser Soft Tissue Surgery: Volume One
Diode Laser Soft Tissue Surgery: Volume Two
Diode Laser Soft Tissue Surgery: Volume Three

These, and other titles, are available at Online Retailers

www.ingramcontent.com/pod-product-compliance
Lightning Source LLC
Chambersburg PA
CBHW060505240426
43661CB00007B/917